Start Your Own

FASHION ACCESSORIES BUSINESS

Additional titles in *Entrepreneur's* **Startup Series**

Start Your Own

Entrepreneur MAGAZINE'S

startup

Start Your Own

FASHION ACCESSORIES BUSINESS

Your Step-by-Step Guide to Success

Entrepreneur Press and Eileen Figure Sandlin

EP
Entrepreneur.
Press

Jere L. Calmes, Publisher
Managing Editor: Marla Markman
Cover Design: Beth Hansen-Winter
Production and Composition: Eliot House Productions

This publication is designed to provide accurate and authoritative information in regard
to the subject matter covered. It is sold with the understanding that the publisher is not
engaged in rendering legal, accounting or other professional services. If legal advice or
other expert assistance is required, the services of a competent professional person
should be sought.

Library of Congress Cataloging-in-Publication Data is available

ISBN-13: 978-1-59918-270-4
ISBN-10: 1-59918-270-X

Printed in Canada

13 12 11 10 09   10 9 8 7 6 5 4 3 2 1

Contents

▲

Chapter 7

Calling in the Professionals 73

Chapter 8

Fashion Central: Your Home Office 81

Chapter 9

Going to the Source 93

Preface

The stock market may tumble. Gas prices may fluctuate wildly. Global warming may yet unleash unprecedented climate changes. But fashion will go on, which could make this the perfect time for you to make a foray into this exciting world as the owner of a fashion accessories business.

Just think of it. Fashion accessories always tend to be in vogue, no matter what the state of the economy. When times are good, people indulge their desire for accessories to add that certain *je ne sais quoi* to every garment in their wardrobe. Then when times are tough, they still buy accessories as a cost-effective way to "bling" up their look when the budget just can't stretch far enough to allow for a new wardrobe. Talk about a win-win situation!

The proof is in the numbers. The Accessories Council, the industry's own national advocacy organization, says that the accessories segment of the overall fashion industry is itself a $30 billion business. That represents a lot of bags and belts, shoes and scarves, baubles and bangles. It also represents a great opportunity for an aspiring entrepreneur like you to connect with trendy fashionistas and cash in on their craving for hip, sassy, classy, and just plain fun fashion accessories.

And there's another huge reason why this is a great time to start a business, and it can be summed up in two words: the internet. You can find everything you need to handcraft or manufacture accessories on the internet, then you can harness its power to find customers eager to buy them. That's another one of those win-win situations that's just too irresistible to ignore.

So in the book you're holding, you'll find the 411 you'll need to launch your own business selling handcrafted jewelry; handbags and tote bags; and/or belts, scarves and hats. Among the topics covered are:

- Exploring the various ways you can enter the accessories industry, from designing, creating and/or manufacturing your own products, to purchasing wholesale accessories and reselling them to retailers
- Determining the best places to sell your merchandise, including brick-and-mortar stores, virtual stores, arts-and-crafts shows, trunk shows, and more
- Setting up a virtual store, from web site to virtual shopping cart
- Locating reliable and reputable sources of raw materials and/or ready-made wholesale goods, both here and abroad
- Creating a demand for your products through targeted marketing efforts that focus on the wants and needs of your prospective customers
- Preparing a detailed business plan to serve as a roadmap to success
- Selecting the best business structure for your new fashion empire
- Finding business professionals whose expertise can help you reach your financial and personal goals
- Drumming up and hiring qualified sales personnel, if needed, to help run the business so you can still have a personal life
- Setting up and equipping an efficient home office
- Establishing a brand and advertising it effectively
- Generating positive press for the business—at no cost to you
- Managing your income and expenses effectively to lay the groundwork for a flourishing and profitable business, while keeping Uncle Sam happy

While this book does delve into all the behind-the-scenes activities necessary to run a business efficiently and effectively, it does not provide instruction on how to handcraft jewelry, how to design kickin' handbags, or how to manufacture the fashion products you intend to sell. That job is best left to the pros—although you will find some resources listed in Chapter 12 that can set you on the right path to getting any instruction you might need.

In addition, throughout this book you'll find words of wisdom from practicing fashion accessories gurus—all of whom are small-business owners who used their love of fashion, tempered by steely determination, to create their own successful ventures. Their insight and advice alone is worth the price of this book—plus you'll find their e-mail addresses listed in the appendix just in case you'd like to ask them a question as you go about setting up your own business.

Now it's your turn. Your success is in the bag—or the bling. So turn the page and go for it!

Accessories
for Success

I t's more fad-driven than possibly any other industry. It's extremely fickle, changing with the seasons and dramatically reflecting both the upswings and downturns of the economy. But it's this unpredictability that makes the $300 billion fashion industry one of the most fascinating and exciting around.

Considering the monetary value of the industry, it's not surprising that there are so many opportunities for creative people interested in forging a career in the field. The industry employs everyone from fashion designers and pattern makers to sewing machine operators and textile stylists, as well as a whole raft of people in ancillary professions, including fashion models, editors and writers; advertising copywriters and publicists; educators—and, of course, the people who sell the fashion items to an adoring public.

In fact, one could argue that boutique owners, visual merchandisers, department-store buyers,and other retail industry professionals are just as influential in the fashion industry equation as the designers themselves. They make merchandising decisions that collectively can make or break a product line. They promote young designers through in-store advertising and promotional sales. They also help build brand loyalty by featuring established favorites, which is an increasingly important function in these days of retail-allegiance shifts among some of the world's best-known designers.

All that Glitters

Fashion accessories command 10 percent of the overall fashion market, or $30 billion, according to the Accessories Council, an organization dedicated to raising awareness of and demand for fashion accessories. Fashion accessories include everything from footwear and handbags to jewelry and watches, gloves and scarves, hats and headbands, belts and ties, wraps and anything else people use to polish their look and create their own style.

This book provides the advice and background you need to start a hip and trendy fashion accessories business. The businesses featured here are grouped into three categories: handcrafted jewelry; handbags and tote bags; belts, scarves, and hats. But it's not unusual in this industry to find accessories businesses that carry a mix of products, particularly when they're sold in a brick-and-mortar or virtual store. However, because it's hard work launching a new business and because product categories have their own unique characteristics, demands, and sources, it's really recommended that you initially focus on a single product line. As you become more familiar with business operations like

Stat Fact
Although there are no available statistics on the number of fashion accessories designers working in the United States today, the U.S. Department of Labor's *Occupational Outlook Handbook, 2008–09 Edition* estimates that fashion designers hold about 20,000 jobs; about 24 percent of them are self-employed.

production, inventory management, and sales, you can entertain the idea of expanding and cross-marketing your product line.

While this book covers advice on how to start a brick-and-mortar retail operation, it's recommended at this stage of your fashion career that you start your business as a homebased virtual or wholesale operation. When you're trying to adjust to a new career with its unfamiliar demands, it's important to keep things as simple as possible, and running a retail store, overseeing employees, and managing vast inventories while still trying to have a personal life is a tall order.

There's another important reason to start as a homebased business: You can get underway with a fairly low investment of capital. Since low and unpredictable cash flow are major challenges faced by new business owners—challenges that have been known to sink even the most intrepid entrepreneur—keeping your expenses as low as possible improves your chances of success.

Entrée to the Industry

No matter where you physically hang your hat, there are several different types of *chapeaux* you can wear as a new fashion business owner. For instance, you can operate as a wholesaler, buying accessories at wholesale cost and selling them directly to retailers, either by calling on them to show your merchandise, using a sales representative to hawk your wares for you, or selling through an online store. Target markets for wholesalers include retail stores of all sizes, including department stores, boutiques and gift stores; industry trade shows (where retail buyers congregate en masse to do their buying); retail stores that take product on consignment; home shopping cable TV networks like QVC and HSN; and even other online accessories retailers like BagBorrowandSteal.com, which is a website that rents high-end handbags to fashion-forward customers by the week or the month. (If you've never seen this website before, go there now—you'll wish you'd thought of this brilliant sales strategy first.)

If you prefer the retail side of the business, you also have plenty of sales options but you'll personally be doing the selling. Among the places you can sell fashion accessories are craft shows, malls, street festivals, and vendor carts; the aforementioned retail stores, which can be brick-and-mortar or virtual; trunk shows (held at your own store or someone else's); home parties; and even eBay, either through auction sales or in an eBay store.

> **Tip...**
>
> **Smart Tip**
> When marketing fashion accessories online, don't forget to target some of your efforts toward men because, according to research by Unity Marketing, they spend the most on luxury fashion items. During the three-month period studied, men spent an average of $2,401 online on fashion items, while women spent $1,527.

On the Block

Y<!-- -->ou might not think that an online auction website like eBay could be the springboard to success as a fashion accessories designer/seller. But don't overlook this easy-to-use and reasonably priced resource when planning your business development strategy—there are eBay millionaires among us who started out exactly as you are starting today: with little more than a dream and a limited budget.

What makes eBay such a remarkable marketplace is its breadth and reach. "*Everyone* is the market on eBay—there is no single demographic to describe it," says Jim "Griff" Griffith, dean of eBay Education. "Your customers are men and women. They're young and old. They live in every country around the world and they come from all economic backgrounds. So you don't have to worry about demographics as long as you use the right keywords and item specifics to describe your item."

The good news is eBay has tutorials and other tools to help you pick those keywords and write the best possible listing. That's critical because there are a lot of listings on eBay: When this book was written, there were 2.4 million listings in the clothing, shoes, and accessories category alone, and 1.2 million listings in the jewelry and watches category.

Rather than discouraging you, those numbers should energize you. There obviously is a big market for fashion accessories on eBay if the numbers are any indication. So go to ebay.com and take the site for a spin. Try listing a few accessories or opening an eBay store. You never know—eBay could be your ticket to worldwide sales and success.

For more information on how to start you own business on eBay, check out Entepreneur's *Start Your Own eBay Business*.

Of course, there's one more important decision you have to make before you jump into the business: You need to decide whether you prefer to sell custom accessories designed and manufactured by yourself or someone you hire, or whether you'll buy them wholesale and resell them. If you're creative, being a designer truly is an exciting way to make a living in this industry. But the manufacturing part of the equation isn't at all creative and, in fact, can be not only expensive but also downright frustrating, with its rigid schedules, production delays, and shipping issues. In addition, many of the most affordable manufacturing facilities are located overseas, typically in the Far East, which means you could encounter language barriers, time zone issues, etc. If all you want to do is create and sell, you may want to skip the manufacturing headaches and stick to custom-designed pieces.

Before you jump into anything, think carefully about your options. Do you enjoy direct customer contact? Then wholesaling to retail customers could be the right career path for you. You might also enjoy selling at street fairs and craft shows, or through home parties. If you're a designer, you'll need good social skills because the onus will be on you to promote your own collection. But if you're more reserved, then an online store could be a better option, assuming you have good organizational and time management skills.

Prospective Clients

As you can see, there are quite a few places where you can sell accessories. Knowing that, you probably can tell that your clientele will fall roughly into three categories:

- *Craft show/street fair customers.* A lot of fashion accessories entrepreneurs and designers wisely start out selling at these local shows as a way to gauge the interest people have in their products. Because the cost to exhibit at such shows is generally quite low, they're good places to meet people, get feedback on your products and prices, and sell some accessories at the same time. But don't let the homespun image fool you—retail buyers have been known to prowl through the bigger shows, as one of the entrepreneurs interviewed for this book learned firsthand—the result of that casual contact was a huge jewelry order for a nationally known retail chain store that essentially launched her fashion accessories career.

  You'll hear more about her in a later chapter. In the meantime, you do need to be aware that for every career-making opportunity that comes along, you'll probably meet a hundred or a thousand looky-loos. But these kinds of grass-roots sales venues are still good places to start to build a loyal clientele while developing essential selling skills. The key to success is to choose the right shows in which to participate. We'll give you some pointers on how to do that later.

- *Wholesale customers.* Anyone who buys your products and resells them at retail prices falls into this category. A retail buyer for a large department chain is a typical wholesale customer, as are the retail buyers who trawl for new and exciting products at industry trade shows. So are the mom-and-pop boutique owners

Beware! You should never, ever sell fashion accessories at wholesale prices directly to the general public, even if you need to liquidate stock or clear out last season's merchandise—even if your friends and family beg. You'll never make any money that way, plus you'll devalue your merchandise in the eyes of your true wholesale customers.

you'll be calling on when you do a grand selling tour. In addition to making personal sales calls on these folks, you can sell to wholesale customers through a website. You just have to make sure the person who contacts you is a genuine wholesale customer and not a retail consumer in disguise.

- *Retail customers.* These are the people who will buy directly from you in a brick-and-mortar store or through your website. Home parties and eBay are also good sources of retail customers. However, a lot of people who sell fashion accessories for a living say it's better to leave the retailing to the department-store chains and boutiques because it's too hard to make a living on onesie-twosie sales unless the price point of the merchandise is extremely high, as it would be if you were selling fine jewelry or designer handbags. Still, selling at retail prices gives you the same kind of insight that going to a craft show yields—albeit at a much higher cost if you're operating out of a brick-and-mortar retail space. This is not to discourage you from retailing if you're a born merchant. But you'll find there are significant challenges that are easy to overlook when you're excited about launching a new business venture.

Through the Ages

Before we delve into the full slate of activities required to launch a fashion accessories business, it's helpful to have some background on exactly how today's love affair with fashion accessories began. It's pretty safe to assume that as long as women have walked the earth, there has been an interest in fashion. While early written records don't exist about how women adorned themselves, there are many extant artifacts and a lot of pictorial evidence to prove that women—and men, for that matter—have always been fashion forward.

Jewelry and Belts

It's believed that the origins of mankind's interest in clothing dates back to around 10,000 B.C. Archeologists have found evidence that the needle and the loom were invented around that time, but it wasn't until the Neolithic period (6,000 B.C.) that humans began to make jewelry, which could be considered the world's first fashion accessories.

Fast-forward 3,000 years. It's well documented that the ancient Egyptians loved cosmetics, fashion, and jewelry, including necklaces, rings, bracelets, and anklets. In fact, Egyptians of all social classes wore jewelry, though of course the ornaments worn by the pharaoh and other members of the elite were costlier and more ornate than those of the lower classes and the peasantry. One reason why jewelry was so popular was because it was believed to have magical powers that offered the wearer spiritual protection or good luck. Tomb paintings also depict Egyptians wearing sashes over simple, pleated kilt-like garments for men or long linen tunics for women, while from the age of puberty children wore hair ornaments and miniature versions of the jewelry their parents wore.

The ancient Romans were also mad for accessories. In particular, upper-class Roman women complemented their attire with highly decorated and costly necklaces, armbands, breast chains, brooches, and even hairnets made of gold.

Over time, ornamentation became even more lavish. In the Middle Ages (around 453 to 1450 A.D.), belts were considered a symbol of wealth and high fashion among noblewomen and often were made of gold-studded leather or plaques of gold that were hinged or sewn to fabric to create elaborately embellished girdles (as belts or sashes used to be called). Women also wore circlets in their hair, as well as bejeweled mantel (cloak) fastenings, brooches, and rings.

Hats and Scarves

Head coverings probably have been worn since the dawn of mankind, but it wasn't until the late 1700s that hats were designed just for women. (Previously, their headwear was influenced by men's styles.) Women's hats first appeared in Milan, Italy, around 1529, giving rise to the term "milliner" for hat makers. They were made of straw and festooned with ribbons. Italian- and Swiss-made straws remained popular until the mid 1800s, when hat makers began using velvet and tulle in their designs.

During the first half of the 19th century, very large bonnets replaced straws and were decorated elaborately with ribbons, flowers and feathers. By the end of the century, however, wide-brimmed hats with flat crowns as well as the toque, a small, brimless hat, caught the fancy of fashionable women. Hats remained popular through the 1950s, when the arrival of ready-to-wear clothing essentially put a lid on the millinery industry. In addition, the stiff, teased hairstyles of the '60s; long, straight styles of the '70s; and wildly tousled hair of the '80s pretty much killed any remaining interest in hats as a fashion accessory.

But there was one place where hats were still popular: the American South, where women continued the Kentucky Derby tradition of donning large and elaborate hats for the festivities. It wasn't until Diana, the Princess of Wales, began to wear hats as a fashion item in the 1990s that widespread interest in fanciful head coverings was revived.

Scarves also have a long history—pun intended—dating back at least as far as ancient Rome. Back then, they were linen cloths called *sudarium* (Latin for "sweat cloth") that were sported by men, who wore them to wipe their faces. Eventually they started knotting longer ones at the waist or wearing them around the neck as a fashion accessory. In addition, Chinese warriors began wearing cloth scarves into battle in the second century B.C. as a way to indicate rank.

Around the 17th century, the French adopted the custom of wearing a neck scarf—ironically enough—from Croatian mercenaries, and renamed the accessory the *cravat*. They remained the trendsetters, and it was a Frenchman, Thierry Hermès, who, in the 1930s, created what is probably the world's most famous scarf. Today, scarves are worn as symbols of religious piety in the Middle East, as sashes and belts, as bright splashes of color over coats, and of course at the throat as protection against the elements.

Handbags

Handbags have also undergone a tremendous metamorphosis over time. They, too, have been part of everyday society for millennia, although what we now call a handbag was little more than a sack as recently as 200 years ago. But we do know that prehistoric people used medicine bags, and fashionable Egyptians were depicted in hieroglyphics with pouches slung around their waists.

The immediate precursor of the modern handbag was known as a *reticule* and debuted as a new fashion accessory during the Regency era of the late 1790s. Previously women carried personal items in "pockets," which were actually cloth bags tied at the waist and worn under the outermost layer of clothing. One of the items they carried in their pockets was a "pocketbook," which was shaped like today's envelope bag and held useful items like thimbles, buttons, and household papers.

> **Fun Fact**
>
> Like women, men carried pocketbooks from about 1740 to 1780, although theirs were generally filled with important papers, coins and currency, and were made of leather. Women's pocketbooks were often made of linen, wool or silk, finished with binding tape, and closed with a metal clasp. Pocketbooks were such important accessories that they often were willed to deserving descendents.

The reticules (or "outside pockets") of the late 18th century were actually more like today's evening bag, and often were made drawstring-style with long strings, ribbons, and feathers. They became popular because women began to adopt the neoclassical style of dress, which had a slimmer silhouette that, of course, would be ruined by bulging pockets worn under skirts. For the first time women also began to carry bags to match their dresses.

By the 1820s reticules had morphed into something more like today's handbag and for the first time were made of leather with decorative embellishments, like buckles. In the early 1900s, the term "handbag" was coined, and they gained prominence as a symbol of a woman's independence since they allowed her to carry whatever she needed wherever she went, rather than relying on a man to do the honors for her.

Stat Fact

The world leaders in the high-end fashion accessories industry are the LVMH Group, which includes Moet Hennessy and Louis Vuitton SA; and PPR SA, owner of Gucci and Yves Saint Laurent. On the jewelry side, Tiffany & Co., Cie, and Bulgari are the world's top three jewelers by revenue.

The mother of today's designer "status bags" is considered to be Coco Chanel, who in 1955 designed the seminal "2.55," a quilted handbag with a chain strap that, in 21st century manifestations, is still considered a must-have by fashionable women.

Handbags are reinvented about every 10 years. For example, clutch bags were introduced around 1930, only to be replaced by shoulder bags during World War II. Today's to-die-for styles are oversized, made of luxurious materials, and have shorter handles and striking hardware. They may be today's most important fashion accessory because they allow women to add a dash of designer style to their look without spending a fortune.

Earnings Potential

Speaking of fortunes, there's a lot of money to be made as a fashion accessories tycoon. However, as with any kind of business startup, you'll have a learning curve, and you could find yourself faced with lean times in the early years of your business. We recommend that you start your business as a part-time venture to learn the fashion ropes. At the very least, it helps to have someone else—a spouse, significant other, or even a parent, depending on your age—who can cover things like the mortgage, groceries, car payments, and health insurance while you set yourself up for success.

Having said that, however, it's important to note that people do make money in this industry. Although statistics don't exist concerning the income potential of fashion accessories entrepreneurs, according to the U.S. Department of Labor's *Occupational Outlook Handbook, 2008–09 Edition*, the average annual earning for salaried fashion designers was $62,610. However, the book goes on to say that some of "the most successful self-employed fashion designers may earn many times the salary of the highest paid salaried designers." Another information source, EducationPortal.com, says that the earnings potential for a successful accessories designer is well over $100,000.

Fun Fact

At Neiman Marcus, where the average handbag sells for $1,200, buyers snapped up a special limited edition Chanel handbag crafted for the store's 100th anniversary in 2007. The price tag was $25,000—and the 25 bags sold out before you could say "Coco Chanel."

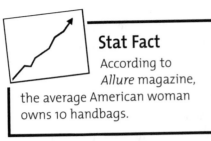

Stat Fact

According to *Allure* magazine, the average American woman owns 10 handbags.

Here's another way to approach the earnings conundrum. The website Payscale.com says that the median salary for a retail store manager with less than one year's experience is $32,412, while the *Occupational Outlook Handbook* pegs the wage of general and operations managers in clothing and clothing accessories stores at $27.16 per hour, or $56,493 per year, based on a 40-hour workweek.

These figures will at least give you an idea of what you might be able to earn. The rest is up to you.

Meet the Entrepreneurs

In the chapters that follow, you'll learn everything you need to know to lay the groundwork for the launch of your new fashion accessories business. Included throughout the book are the insights and views of a number of experienced fashion accessories business owners who generously shared their knowledge about their own operations. This is firsthand insight you'll find useful now, as you start making business decisions, as well as later, when you are looking for new ideas and inspiration. The entrepreneurs you'll hear from include:

- *Ruta Fox, president and founder of Divine Diamonds, New York City.* Fox is the creator of the Ah Ring, a diamond and white gold ring designed for and targeted to single women. She has 15 years of writing experience in the advertising, branding, marketing, and public relations industries, and has been published in magazines like *Vanity Fair, Health, Seventeen,* and *Us Magazine.* She became a jewelry entrepreneur pretty much by accident in 2001 after she started wearing a small diamond pinkie ring she bought for herself and was inundated with requests from her friends for a similar ring. Concurrently her doctor advised her to find something to do besides sitting at a computer writing all day, so she started selling the Ah (which stands for "available" and "happy") ring as a way to make money while looking for a new career.

- *Reagan Hardy and Emmie Howard, co-owners of Southern Proper in Atlanta.* These two Southern belles unabashedly admit that they have always loved two things: Southern men and fashion. These loves became the impetus for founding a business that manufactures and sells a "Southern preppy" brand of men's furnishings, including neckties and bowties, formalwear sets, "drawls" (aka boxer shorts), knit shirts, and hats and visors. They also recently started selling

Do You Have What It Takes?

Being the owner of a small business usually sounds like a dream job to most people. After all, you're captain of your own ship. You can make decisions without a snarling boss breathing down your neck, and you can work as little or as much as you wish.

Oh, wait—scratch that last one. When you're self-employed, you may find yourself working morning, noon, and night ... and on weekends and holidays and during vacations. The reality is, when you're a Lone Ranger you do whatever it takes to keep the business going and the bills paid.

But running a business takes more than just dogged commitment and time. You also must:

○ *Be disciplined.* That means ignoring the call of your tennis racket on a warm summer day or the pleas of your children to go skating on a frosty winter day. It also means sticking to a schedule and finishing projects no matter what else goes undone.

○ *Be a self-motivated self-starter.* Entrepreneurs—especially those who are homebased—must play well alone. You won't have co-workers with whom to chat over coffee or a secretary to do your photocopying or make runs to the post office. It's all up to you.

○ *Be prepared.* Do you have enough money set aside to pay your personal bills while you build the business? Business startups are notorious for being unprofitable for a few years, so you'll need resources to survive.

○ *Have a vision.* In the beginning, it's best to start with a simple goal, like selling fashion jewelry online. But you need to have a plan. Will you move into manufacturing? Will you add hats to your scarf line? How soon? Entrepreneurs are always thinking—or scheming—about reaching the next level.

women's headbands and plan to expand their line of women's accessories in the near future.

Hardy holds a bachelor's degree in journalism and mass communication from the University of North Carolina, while Howard holds a bachelor's degree in business/marketing from Brenau University Women's College. Not surprisingly, Howard is Southern Proper's operations expert, while Hardy focuses on sales and marketing.

- *David Kulaas, owner of Kulisilk in Golden, Colorado.* Kulaas is a former Air Force fighter pilot who, in 2005, parlayed an interest in nature photography into a wholesale silk scarf manufacturing company because he wanted something to do after retiring from a 35-year career as a stockbroker with Merrill Lynch. ("It keeps me out of the pool halls," he says.) He uses his own photos of Colorado wildflowers as inspiration for his designs, then has the scarves manufactured in China. His accessories are sold primarily in small boutiques in Martha's Vineyard, Massachusetts; Seattle, Washington; Santa Monica, California; and Scottsdale, Arizona.

- *Brooke Sobel, owner of Sobella in San Francisco, California.* A graduate of the University of Southern California, Sobel is a former kindergarten teacher, public relations executive, and recruiter. She entered the fashion accessories industry as a jewelry designer in 1999 following a trip to Costa Rica, where she was inspired by a woman she met there who was making jewelry and handbags. After designing jewelry for five years as well as a handbag with a removable handle that could be worn as a necklace, Sobel realized her true love was handbag design and began to pursue that line of business full time in 2004. Her collections, which she describes as both funky and chic, can be found at department stores and boutiques worldwide, including Bloomingdale's, Nordstrom, Takashimaya, Harvey Nichols, and more.

- *Donna von Hoesslin, designer and owner of Betty Belts and Betty B. in Ventura, California.* A former Berlin socialite who was "at the top of the fashion scene," as she phrases it, von Hoesslin has had an eclectic life. During two decades in Europe, she worked jobs ranging from waitress to translator to fashion designer (with her own cut-and-sew business). After returning to Southern California, this avid surfer started her company in 2001 to produce unique, handmade belts, jewelry, and accessories that are ocean-inspired, ethically made, and sweatshop-free. She uses reclaimed and recycled components in her designs, which makes the pieces both sustainable and affordable. She also supports many different causes, including environmental groups, at-risk youth organizations, women's surfing, and the female artisans in Bali who so competently make her products.

- *Liza Sonia Wallach, owner of LIZASonia in Oakland, California.* This handcrafted jewelry designer founded her company in 2003. Born in Guadalajara, Mexico, Wallach has always considered herself an artist, although following graduation from the University of California Berkeley with a degree in psychology and biology, she held various executive-level positions, including COO of a privately held international company. During a two-year solo trip around the world, she finally explored her inner designer and launched her own business after returning home. Today her eye-catching designs are sold at Nordstrom and other fine stores.

Handcrafted
Jewelry Business

From baubles to beads, bails to bracelets, jewelry design and crafting are creative, satisfying and just plain fun ways to while away your free time. But when you make the transition from creating handcrafted jewelry for fun to selling it for profit, there's a new dynamic involved. Suddenly you have to create a cohesive collection of items. You must select supplies

▲

with an eye toward price point. You have to complete projects on a strict schedule. You also must create a lot of the same items, which frankly can feel more like working on an assembly line and be a lot less fun than doing whatever pleases you at any given moment.

That's the downside. The *up*side is that you get to play with beads and cabochons and findings, and make money at it. It doesn't get any better than that.

And there's a huge market primed and waiting for the necklaces, bracelets, earrings, rings, anklets, cufflinks, and other jewelry items you create. In a recent year, American consumers spent more than $62 billion on buying jewelry and watches, according to the *Jewelry and Market Watch Report*. That was a 6.5 percent increase in sales over the previous year. In addition, the luxury jewelry market had a double-digit sales increase, according to a market research study conducted by Unity Marketing, a boutique market research firm. So whether you aspire to be the next Jennifer Kirk— a leading designer of crystal and beaded jewelry—or the next David Yurman—the

Staking Your Claim

Design theft is a regrettable byproduct of creative pursuits like jewelry design. As soon as you display your fabulous new designs at a trade show, a street fair or on the internet, you're bound to see duplicates popping up on other people's tables or websites (no doubt because they don't possess a shred of creativity in their souls to do better).

So what can you do about that? Actually, you might be surprised to know that your designs are automatically protected by law. As soon as you create an "original work of authorship," as the U.S. Copyright Office calls it, it's protected by common law copyright. Your work would fall into the "pictorial, graphic and sculptural works" category, and you're automatically allowed to use the © symbol to let everyone know it.

Unfortunately, people often don't heed common law copyright and gleefully knock off whatever strikes their fancy. So if you really want to have legal recourse against shysters who copy your jewelry and sell it for profit (translation: if you want to sue the counterfeit Manolo Blahniks right off them), you can file for an officially recognized copyright in the jewelry design category. Simply go to the U.S. Copyright Office website at copyright.gov, fill out Form CO, fork over the $45 filing fee, and you'll be in business—or at least, your competitors will be out of business while you hold the copyright, which is in effect for the remainder of your life, plus 70 years after you've shuffled off to Jewelry Heaven. That should be long enough to get scurvy thieves to go looking elsewhere for creative work to steal.

renowned luxury jewelry designer—you'll find there are plenty of fashion-forward women (and the men who buy jewelry for them) primed and ready for your designs.

There are a lot of ways you can sell your jewelry, as you'll discover in Chapter 10. For now, it's enough to know that the information in this chapter applies to any manifestation of the business you choose to establish, from a homebased virtual or retail operation to a brick-and-mortar store, or even both.

By the way, we also recognize that you may not be a jewelry designer, but rather an entrepreneur interested in selling handcrafted jewelry purchased from designers or manufacturers. There's plenty of advice for you in this book, too, including information in Chapter 9 on how to manufacture jewelry designed by others and where to buy wholesale accessories for resale. If the information in this chapter doesn't apply to you, feel free to go on to Chapter 5, which covers market research. We'll meet you there later.

A Day in the Life

Designing and creating jewelry may be your *raison d'etre* for becoming an entrepreneurial jewelry designer/seller, but as a small-business owner you'll have a number of behind-the-scenes tasks unrelated to jewelry making that you'll need to handle to keep the business running. To begin with, you'll probably spend a substantial amount of time on the phone, talking to jewelry components suppliers, as well as answering e-mails and attending to accounts payable/receivable yourself or talking to your accountant about them. You'll research new suppliers, both online and in person, follow up on promising supplier leads, and visit suppliers' places of business whenever possible to see what they offer live and in person. You'll order supplies and figure out where to squeeze the budget to pay for them. You'll be the creative genius who dreams up and executes brilliant advertising and marketing campaigns designed to spread the word about your jewelry. And finally, if your collection takes off and you have so many orders you can't possibly process them all yourself, you'll oversee the contract or temporary help you'll bring in to help with fulfillment and shipping.

Other administrative tasks you can expect to handle fall into several categories, including:

- *Sales.* Naturally, since you're currently unknown on the fashion jewelry circuit, you'll have to spend a fair amount of time each week persuading retailers that your products

Bright Idea

When you hit on a winning design that you plan to make over and over again, write down all the components in a "recipe book" so you know exactly what goes into each piece and how much time you spend putting it together. This also saves you a lot of time when you're ordering materials and calculating the price of each item.

are must-haves in their stores. The best way to do this, of course, is to make personal sales calls because retailers love to meet new designers and because there's no substitute for showing off your products in their full glory. In addition to taking your entire jewelry collection along to display to interested retailers, you'll also need a line sheet and possibly a press kit (both of which are discussed in Chapter 13). Once you've caught the interest of retailers, you'll have to stay in contact with them to keep them informed about pricing, delivery schedules, and other pertinent information. Finally, once retailers agree to carry your products, you'll have to follow up with them constantly, both to find out how the merchandise is doing as well as to write up reorders and keep them informed about new products you've added to your collection.

- *Order processing/fulfillment.* In the beginning, this shouldn't be too difficult to handle yourself because you won't have a ton of orders to process right out of the box. In addition to processing orders that come in via the internet or fax, you'll have to produce invoices for each account, place the jewelry into the packaging you've selected (possibly jewelry boxes or pouches), box up the order, then either deliver the boxes to the post office or a shipping company like UPS or Mailboxes Etc., or call for a pickup. Eventually, of course, you may find that the fulfillment and processing functions are taking up too much valuable time from sales and product development, and you'll have to turn over these tasks to others.

- *Website administration/maintenance.* Whether you plan to sell jewelry through a virtual store on your website or just display your merchandise in cyberspace so retailers can see it before ordering, website administration and maintenance will be crucial daily activities. On the maintenance side, you'll have to post new product information and pictures, then remove or update information. The administration part will include downloading those orders mentioned earlier, responding to requests for information, and otherwise keeping in touch with prospects.

- *Store operation.* If your goal is to open a brick-and-mortar jewelry store, the fun has just begun. In addition to all the other tasks mentioned above, you'll have to staff the store, stock the shelves, handle the cash register, protect the merchandise from sticky-fingered looky-loos, and otherwise keep the business running. And of course, when you're not there, you're not making money, so you'll have to come to terms with the idea that your life is not really your own anymore and you'll probably have to forgo vacations and days off, especially in the early days.

While we would never discourage an entrepreneur from reaching for his/her dream, we suggest that you defer opening a store until you've been in business for a while. Not that it's not possible to open a store right away. Liza Sonia

Wallach, the Oakland, California, jewelry designer, successfully runs her hand-crafted jewelry operation out of a 250-square-foot store in a shopping center. However, she started in an even smaller space—just 100 square feet—for which she paid $400 a month, considerably lower than the going rate of $8 to $9 per square feet.

Normally, it's a good idea to wait a couple of years before making the plunge into retail store management because it gives you time to learn the ropes of running a business and develop an outstanding product line without the considerable expense of a retail Sword of Damocles hanging over your head.

A better way to try out your merchandise in a retail environment would be to hold a trunk show. A trunk show is a special sale of short duration (as short as one afternoon to as long as a day or two) that's usually held at a retail store. During the sale, a designer's entire collection is displayed. It's a great way to gauge interest in your merchandise, although of course you do have to convince a boutique or other retail store owner to host the show. You'll find more information about trunk shows in Chapter 10.

- *Jewelry design/handcrafting.* Oh, yes, amid all this activity you'll have to find time to design and create handcrafted jewelry. But of course, the more stock you have, the more you can sell, so you'll naturally want to set aside the lion's share of your time for this important task. One way to get a lot of merchandise into the market is to create a line of production jewelry; i.e., jewelry that's manufactured by a company to your specifications. You'll find advice about how to do that in Chapter 9.

Tools of the Trade

If you've been designing or making jewelry as a hobbyist for a while, you might already have many or all the tools and toys you need to ply your new professional craft. But just in case you're new to this profession or you haven't previously indulged your inner jewelry designer completely, here's a list of the tools and supplies you may need:

- *Pliers*
  - Chain nose: for gripping and bending wire
  - Crimping: to give crimp beads or tubes a round rather than flat shape
  - Curved tip flat nosed: to make wrapping easier from all angles
  - Curved tip round nosed: to make wire wrapping easier
  - Flat nose: all-purpose pliers
  - Long round nose: for wrapping wire
  - Nylon flat jaw: for working with wire that's easily scratched or dented

▲

      – Split ring: for opening and holding split rings

- *Tweezers*
  - Bent nose: for grabbing small objects while beading
  - Long utility: for holding beads and pearls
  - Thin tip: for knotting and other applications
- *Needles*
  - Beading needles in assorted sizes
  - Big eye curved
  - Big eye flexible
  - Collapsible
  - Twisted beading
  - Self-threading
- *Adhesives*
  - Amazing GOOP: for use with ceramic, glass, metal, and other materials
  - E6000: industrial strength, washer/dryer-safe craft and jewelry adhesive
  - Epoxy paste: for repairing and filling
  - G-S HYPO cement: for gluing stretchy cords and other craft materials
- *Miscellaneous*
  - Bead design board: with grooves to hold multiple strands at once and compartments to store beads and supplies while you're working
  - Beading loom: for weaving intricate items
  - Beading tray: to hold tools and other items to prevent them from rolling off your work surface
  - Bead reamer: to enlarge or smooth out unevenly drilled holes in beads
  - Calipers: for measuring in millimeters and centimeters
  - Finger thimble: to protect against sharp objects like needles
  - Jump ring tool: for making it easier to open and close jump rings
  - Hands-free magnifier: for crafters with "mature vision" or for seeing tiny components clearly
  - Mini snips: for cutting beading wire and decorative beading thread
  - Pearl reamer: to enlarge or smooth out unevenly drilled holes in pearls
  - Wire cutter: for cutting craft wire and other stringing materials
- *Beads*
  - Acrylic
  - Bone
  - Bumpers

- Cabachons
- Clay
- Cubic zirconia
- Czech glass
- Dichroic
- Fimo
- Furnace
- Gemstone beads
- Glass (bicone, cube, round)
- Japanese treasure beads
- Lampwork
- Metal
- Miracle
- Pearl
- Seed and bugle
- Shell
- Spacers
- Swarovski crystals
- Turquoise
- Wood and nut
- *Findings*
  - Bails
  - Charms
  - Connectors
  - Crimp beads and tubes
  - Crimp covers
  - Crimp hook and eyes
  - C-ring clasp
  - Earring backs
  - Earring wires
  - Fold-over clasps
  - Head pins
  - Hooks & eyes
  - Jump rings
  - Lobster claw clasp

Bright Idea

Wearing your own jewelry pieces is like free advertising. In fact, Liza Sonia Wallach, the Oakland, California, jewelry designer, got the confidence to start her business after she wore handcrafted pieces she had designed to society gala events, and women who saw them asked if they could buy them right off her neck when they found out she had created them.

- Pin backs
- Spring rings
- Toggle clasps
- Watch faces
- *Stringing materials*
  - Bead stringing wire (7, 19 and 49 strand)
  - Jewelry wire
  - Leather cord
  - Silk bead cord
  - Poly nylon bead cord
- *Metals*
  - Copper
  - Gold (10K, 14K)
  - Gold filled
  - Gold plate (24K electroplate)
  - Silver plate
  - Sterling silver
  - Vermeil
- *Packaging/tagging*
  - Pouches
  - Jewelry boxes
  - Reclosable polybags

Competition

The main competition for a startup jewelry designer is usually found at craft shows and street fairs, because aspiring designers often start out selling that way. To a lesser extent, department stores and boutiques in your market are your competitors, too, if they carry handcrafted items, although at this point in your new career they're actually on a higher competitive tier. Also, cable TV retailers like QVC and HSN, online auction houses like eBay, and other virtual jewelry stores could be considered competition because they're open 24/7. The good news is you can make a good

 Beware!
The typical retail markup for jewelry is a factor of two or three, but sometimes you'll have to price your pieces at up to five times your cost to cover overhead (if you have a store) or transportation costs to the sales venue. But be careful—at the end of the day you don't want to have a lot of pretty pieces and no rent money.

run at breaking into all these sales channels once your business is up and running. You'll find out how in Chapter 10.

Setting Prices

According to craft and jewelry experts, the general rule for pricing jewelry is to add up your costs, then multiply them by a factor of two for wholesale pricing and three for retail pricing. Thus, a bracelet you make for $6 would cost $12 if you sell it wholesale or $18 retail if you sell it in your own virtual or brick-and-mortar store.

Now that probably sounds pretty easy, but unfortunately, there are a lot of variables that can affect that price, not the least of which is how much the customer is willing to pay for the item. For instance, let's say you want to price that bracelet mentioned above at $18 retail. But when you get to the street fair where you're exhibiting, you discover that every other handcrafted bracelet on display around you is priced at $15—and many of them are selling for $12 by the time the bargaining ends . . . you can imagine how well your $18 bracelet will sell.

Which brings us to another way to figure out how to price your jewelry: You should take a comparison shopping trip among your competitors. Be sure to try the internet to figure out what the going price is for items that are similar to yours.

On the other hand, let's say you're planning to sell your jewelry wholesale to retailers like department stores and boutiques, or through a sales representative. (More on how to do that in Chapter 10.) You may have to cut the price of that bracelet down much closer to your cost—say, to $8 or $9—so the retailer can make a profit when it marks up the bracelet to retail price. Now you're probably thinking that's not a very good way to make money. But although you may make less money per item, you should be able to make up the difference in volume. Better to make $2 per bracelet and sell 100 of them than to make $6 per item and sell four.

Naturally, one of the best ways to keep costs down and profits up is to use the most cost-effective components you can

Cultivating Corporate Accounts

Looking for a short-term, surefire way to ramp up sales volumes? Try pitching your bling to corporate accounts.

Corporate accounts are wonderful customers because so many people can see your jewelry at one time, rather like at a craft or trade show. You simply display the goods in a temporary "store" in the company's cafeteria or other employee gathering spot, preferably during lunchtime. In addition to being able to sell lots of jewelry, you'll find that corporations are great places to gain exposure and start building a loyal client base through word-of-mouth. And here's a bonus: You can drive your new customers to your website after you leave simply by printing your web address on your bags or jewelry pouches.

To find a company that might be interested in hosting a "jewelry party," call the human resources department at large corporations and ask to speak to a member of the employee activities team. Be sure to inquire about the male-to-female employee ratio when you call, and time your sale around gift-giving holidays, such as Christmas, Hanukkah, and Mother's Day.

You'll be astounded at how well this strategy works. One jewelry company we know of works the hospital circuit in a major metropolitan area, selling thousands of dollars worth of jewelry during a single visit of about 10 hours (to catch two different shifts). As a goodwill gesture, the owner donates a percentage of the gross sales to the hospital, which of course endears her to management and virtually assures an open door for future sales.

Naturally, you'll have to arrive with a *lot* of jewelry to sell. You may also need to bring contractors to help handle sales. But the financial rewards can be fantastic.

without sacrificing quality. Let's say you found some really outstanding crystal beads that you'd like to use in a necklace design. But the price point per bead will make your necklaces 20 percent more expensive to produce than usual. So if you're really sold on using those fabulous beads, try cutting costs elsewhere, like by substituting a less expensive clasp or making the necklace one inch shorter so your bead and wire costs will be lower.

Of course, the cost of your labor also should be included in the price you charge. But that can get sticky on lower priced items. As an example, let's say that you worked one hour on a piece and you'd like to earn at least $10 an hour. You'd have to add $10 to the cost of the piece to accommodate the hourly wage, which on that $6 bracelet would take the cost up to $22 if you sold it wholesale ($10 labor cost + your $12 wholesale cost, or $28 if you sold it retail on your website ($10 labor cost + your $18 retail cost). The trouble is you'd better make sure the item is worth $28 if you go that high, or no one will buy.

For more insight on pricing your products, refer to Viki Lareau's book, *Marketing and Selling Your Handmade Jewelry: The Complete Guide to Turning Your Passion Into Profit* (Interweave Press), it puts another spin on pricing in understandable terms that you might find helpful.

Startup Expenses

You can start a handcrafted jewelry business for just a few thousand dollars, as Wallach did, although she says it is also possible to launch a jewelry business for as little as $500. Her store came later, so the cost to run it (rent and utilities) didn't figure into her early budget.

You, too, can keep your startup costs low if you launch your company as a home-based business that sells through any sales channel *except* your own retail store. However, because we know that there will be at least some readers who will be interested in opening their own jewelry emporium, we have included sample startup costs for two fictitious businesses on page 24. The business with the lowest expenses, Phyllis Phashions, is a small homebased jewelry design business operated by the owner. She sells handcrafted necklaces on her website and through several local boutiques. The business with the higher expenses, Gem Dreams, operates out of a small strip-mall location and has one employee (the owner). The owner sells one-of-a-kind 14K gold and gemstone jewelry and takes commissions for custom pieces. Even though she can charge more for her jewelry, the significant impact of monthly rent payments on her business is oh-so-obvious.

In addition, you'll find a worksheet on page 25 that you can use to estimate your own startup costs, which you can start penciling in as you read through this book.

Sample Startup Expenses: Handcrafted Jewelry Business

Item	Phyllis Phashions	Gem Dreams
Mortgage/rent (first six months)		$6,000
Leasehold improvements ($10 to $15 per square foot; 600-square-foot space)		$6,000
Office equipment, furniture, supplies	$1,845	$6,152
Jewelry-making tools, supplies, packaging	$500	$2,000
Business licenses (estimated)	$100	$100
Phone (line installation charges)	$40	$150
P.O. box (first six months)	$54	$54
Employee wages and benefits (first six months)		
10 events x $100 per event		
Startup advertising (3% of projected revenue)	$720	$1,200
Legal services (startup package)		$900
Accounting services*		$500
Vehicle (first six months' travel expenses)	$600	
Insurance (annual cost)	$500	$500
Market research	$250	$500
Membership dues		$510
Publications (annual subscriptions) and books	$50	$100
Online service (broadband)	$99	$99
Website design	$1,000	$2,000
Web hosting, domain name	$10	$10
Subtotal	$5,768	$26,775
Miscellaneous expenses (roughly 10% of subtotal)	$600	$2,600
Total	**$6,368**	**$29,375**

*The low-end business uses QuickBooks to keep track of expenses; the high-end business uses an accountant to set up the books.

Startup Expenses Worksheet

Item	
Mortgage/rent (first six months)	$
Leasehold improvements	$
Office equipment, furniture, supplies	$
Jewelry-making tools, supplies, packaging	$
Business licenses (estimated)	$
Phone (line installation charges)	$
P.O. box (first six months)	$
Employee wages and benefits (first six months)	$
Startup advertising (3% of projected revenue)	$
Legal services	$
Accounting services*	$
Vehicle (first six months' travel expenses)	$
Insurance (annual cost)	$
Market research	$
Membership dues	$
Publications (annual subscriptions) and books	$
Online service (broadband)	$
Website design	$
Web hosting, domain name	$
Subtotal	$
Miscellaneous expenses (roughly 10% of subtotal)	$
Total	**$**

3

Handbag
Business

They have names like "Animalier" and "Ritz Fizz." They run the gamut from luxe to loopy (in a good way, of course), and come in all sizes and materials. And they certainly are ubiquitous—there isn't a woman alive who doesn't carry one. OK, there actually are some women in the Western world who don't tote a handbag the size of Oregon, but they are definitely in the minority—and who knows, you may be able to convert them into devoted members of the Purse Brigade with your innovative, chic, or funky handbag designs.

The fact is, handbags have been a hot-hot-hot fashion accessory for years, spawning a $7 billion industry and fueling an escalating market for status bags, or those purses with the astronomical price tags at Barneys, Saks, and other upscale retailers. The lust for luxe even spawned the brilliantly conceived online retailer BagBorrowandSteal.com, which rents high-end bags by the week and by the month to eager fashionistas.

However, according to analysts, there has been some softening of the designer handbag market. The stock research firm Telsey Advisory Group reports that the U.S. market for handbags was expected to increase only 15 percent in a recent year, down from the 28 percent increase of just a few years before. But there continues to be a strong market for more reasonably priced bags starting at $100, so much so that high-end designers like Stella McCartney are teaming up with handbag makers to create more affordable high-style bags. "The whole phenomenon has changed," said Barneys New York fashion director Julie Gilhart in *The New York Times*. "Our customers seem to be looking for something more interesting. They don't want to spend money on something everyone else has."

You'd never know that judging by the mass-market department store chains like Target, which carries a line of beautiful Gryson handbags in the $40 range, including an oversized zip satchel that has the same distinctive look as the $725 Gryson satchel sold at Nieman Marcus. Meanwhile, over at Kohl's, a "Simply Vera" Vera Wang clear tote runs $89, while a faux patent leather tuxedo-style clutch bag is $79.

What all this means for you is that there is a healthy market for aspiring "indie" handbag designers, especially those who design in the moderate price range, or what we'll call the $200 to $350 price point. This chapter will give you insight into the life of a handbag designer. Of course, if you're planning to be a handbag wholesaler or retailer rather than a designer, you'll find the information in this chapter interesting, but perhaps not as useful as the info in Chapter 10, which covers the type of business you're establishing. Feel free to skip ahead if you wish.

A Day in the Life

Quite naturally, your main purpose in life when starting your handbag business will be to design and sew bags. But there's more to running a handbag business than sitting at a computer or drawing board and designing the world's next bestselling bag. Among the other tasks you'll have to undertake on a daily or regular basis to keep the business humming along are:

- *Handling front office tasks.* This includes answering the phone and e-mail, opening the mail, handling paperwork, and attending to accounts receivable/payable

Sew Helpful

Handbag designers often start out with a sewing machine, a grand dream, and a fervent desire to make all their bags themselves. But even if your bags are high end—say, $500 and up—you'll never make a fortune toiling alone. Eventually, you'll need help with the sewing and construction.

If you live in one of the country's fashion centers, you can go to the local fashion design school and hire students to help you with the sewing. Community colleges and vocational schools everywhere often have fashion design programs as well, so you're not out of luck if you don't live where the Beautiful People roam. Check out fabric stores like Joann etc., which usually employ professional sewing teachers who might be interested in moonlighting. Finally, consult the trusty phone book, where you'll find listings for tailors and people who do mending for a living and can provide competent, skilled help.

(or huddling with your accountant to keep the books straight). You'll also be in charge of advertising and marketing your bags and your business.

- *Photographing bags and writing product descriptions.* You'll need to do this for your website and line sheets (leave-behind sales sheets that describe your products in detail for prospective retail customers). You may wish to leave the photography to a professional, but you certainly can write the product descriptions yourself. Keep them short and sweet, and be sure to include pertinent information like materials used, color, size and product number.

- *Processing internet orders.* These could be orders from retailers if you'll be selling wholesale, or from customers who visit your site and are instantly smitten with your brilliant designs. In addition to retrieving orders, you'll have to process credit card payments or personal checks, print receipts, and package merchandise so it can be shipped out.

- *Performing website maintenance.* This is a crucial job whether you're relying on your website as a sales channel or simply as an information site for retail customers. You'll have to download photos and descriptions of your products, constantly remove outdated information, and otherwise keep the site up-to-date. You'll want to be sure you ask your web designer to create a website template you can easily update yourself, or else you'll be constantly giving away cash to have someone do it for you.

- *Researching sources.* Since fashion is so fleeting and fickle, you'll be constantly looking for new and exciting materials for your handbag designs. In addition, you'll need to be on the lookout for suppliers that can provide the best quality at the best price. The internet is a great place to start your search, but the New York and Los Angeles wholesale garment districts and the textile events they hold are often better sources because they have a wider selection and competitive prices. You'll either have to visit the source personally, or order catalogs, swatches, and samples to see what's new.

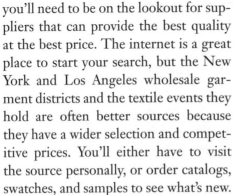

Smart Tip

Although you can use stock numbers or generic labels to catalog your handbags, you should come up with evocative names instead. Use them on your line sheet to catch the attention of buyers and editors, and as a first step toward building your own distinctive brand.

- *Ordering materials.* Once you've located your sources, be prepared to spend, spend, spend. Be sure to keep good records of what you're ordering, where it's coming from, and when it's due to arrive to prevent order duplication.

- *Manufacturing your products.* As a fledgling entrepreneur, you'll probably want to handcraft your products rather than manufacture them in a factory, mostly because the cost of manufacturing can be out of the budget of a startup operation. In addition, handcrafting also means you're in control of the production process and can turn out a high-quality product.

    Of course, even though we don't expect you to become a manufacturing maven this early in your career, if you happen to land a big order, you would need to become a manufacturing expert in a hurry. You'll find information about how to locate a factory and what to do with it in Chapter 10.

- *Running a retail store.* We really don't recommend starting a new handbag business out of a retail space because it's so expensive and time-consuming to be a store owner, but if you do plan to go that route, you'll have a lot of additional responsibilities. They include, but are not limited to, staffing the store, overseeing employees (if you don't go it alone), handling money, keeping the store tidy, overseeing loss prevention (or more bluntly, providing security for your merchandise)—and oh, yes, designing and handcrafting your inventory. So the bottom line is, if you really want to have enough time to develop a signature line of products and create a brand, keep your business homebased and sell virtually and/or wholesale—at least in the beginning.

If you're not a designer and instead will import or purchase handbags domestically rather than making them yourself, then a retail store might make more sense for you. You'll find more information about how to establish and run a retail store in Chapter 10.

In the Bag

There's a vast variety of handbag and tote bag styles. They include:

- *Bucket bag.* Tall bag roughly shaped like a bucket, with a small bottom and a wider top that's often left open
- *Clutch.* Rectangular bag without straps or handles; meant to be carried in the hand or under the arm
- *Diaper bag.* All-purpose, oversized bag used for just about anything, including baby paraphernalia if the fashionistas haven't snapped them all up
- *Duffle bag.* All-purpose bag that's usually longer than it is wide; often used for toting sports equipment and other gear
- *Evening bag.* Small bag, handheld or with a decorative handle, and often embellished with sequins, beads, or other decorations
- *Frame bag.* Type of purse with a support frame to give it structure
- *Hobo.* Slouchy, medium-to-large, unstructured handbag that resembles a "U" when dangled by its handle
- *Laptop bag.* Bag specially designed to carry a laptop and its accessories
- *Man bag.* Spare and conservative bag, often in leather and with many compartments, that's masculine enough for a guy to carry; styles range from duffels to briefcases
- *Messenger bag.* Bag with a long strap meant to be worn across the body
- *Pet bag.* For carrying your best friend with you everywhere you go, whether it's a good idea or not (think Paris Hilton)
- *Satchel.* Bag with a flat bottom, top closure and short handle(s) meant to be carried on the arm
- *Tote bag.* Large, open-top bag with two handles

Tools of the Trade

Among the tools and supplies you'll need to design and make handbags are:

- *Industrial sewing machine.* You can start out with a standard home sewing machine, but you should graduate to an

Fun Fact

A serger (aka overlock machine) is an invaluable tool for production sewing. It uses four to five spools of thread but no bobbin (lower) thread. Instead, looper threads lock together at the seam line, forming a flat stitch. Sergers operate at a speed of 1,500 stitches per minute or higher, which makes short work of handbag construction projects.

Leather Primer

Not all leather is suitable for handbags or belts. Here's a quick primer on the types of leather you're likely to run across as you investigate materials for your merchandise:

○ *Full-grain or top-grain leather.* This is the top grade of leather that's used for both fashion apparel and accessories and furniture. The terms refer to the epidermis (skin) of a hide that has had the hair removed but has not been "corrected" to remove imperfections. This makes the hide more durable and allows it to "breathe," which is why it's most appropriate for apparel.

○ *Corrected-grain leather.* This is a type of top-grain leather that has been sanded or buffed to remove imperfections. It's considered to be of inferior quality to top-grain leather and is often dyed (or pigmented) to hide corrections or imperfections. However, it is a suitable midrange leather for many purposes, including handbags.

○ *Split leather.* This is made from the inner, more fibrous layers of a hide and is more fragile than top-grain leather. Split leather is used to create suede, which is also less durable than top-grain leather. Some manufacturers use special techniques to make suede appear to be more costly full-grain leather.

○ Patent leather. This has been treated to give it a hard, glossy finish. It usually has a plastic or lacquer coating and is ideal for handbags, belts, and footwear.

○ *Vachetta leather.* Popularized by designer Louis Vuitton, this is used for the trim on handbags and luggage.

○ *Belting leather.* Originally used to make pulley belts, belting leather is thick and has a firm, smooth finish. It's often used in luxury products like handbags so it's not necessary to use a frame to give them shape.

industrial model as soon as possible because it's much better suited to handle high-volume sewing and is heavy duty enough to sew on tough materials like leather and vinyl.

• *Serger.* Type of sewing machine for overcasting seams on fabrics that ravel, including cotton and taffeta

• *Basic sewing tools and notions.* Including shears, pinking shears, seam ripper, marking tools, measuring tools, awl (for punching holes in leather), tailor's chalk, pins, thread, etc.

- *Handles.* In various materials, shapes, and sizes
- *Bag frame.* Internal component used to give a bag shape
- *Handbag bottom.* To support or stiffen the bottom of a bag
- *Fabric.* Anything from upholstery fabric to sateen, silk, taffeta, cotton, or anything else that strikes your fancy; purchased by the yard
- *Leather and suede.* For virtually any style of handbag (see "Leather Primer" on page 32 for a list of leather options)
- *Embellishments.* Everything from leather cord to sequins, beads, or whatever else will define your signature style
- *Cord.* For drawstrings, piping, etc.
- *Closures.* Buckles, frogs, snaps, buttons, D-rings, etc.
- *Sketchpad.* For designing and recording design details
- *Software.* If you're adept at using Photoshop or Illustrator, you'll probably want to use it to design your bags. But another option is the Handbag Vector Edition from Amethyst Handbag Library (thehandbagresource.com/index.ptp). This marvelous program has handbag silhouettes and other components that can be mixed and matched to inspire you to achieve great things.

Selling Wholesale

One of the best ways to make money in handbag design is to sell your products at wholesale to retailers because it then becomes their responsibility to sell the products to real, live customers. However, this is not as simple as it might seem. It becomes your job to convince buyers that your product is exactly what they want and that the price point you've set is reasonable and fair.

Usually what happens is you'll call on a retail store (yes, you personally will be making these sales calls unless your budget allows you to hire a sales rep) and show handbag samples. Sometimes you can just walk in the door and talk to the buyer, but if you're trying to break into a department-store chain or an upscale shop, you must make an appointment first. When you do get an appointment, you'll show samples, plus you'll give the buyer your line sheet, which basically is a price list that may include color photos of every handbag you carry in every available color (more on line sheets in Chapter 13). This is a lot more efficient than trying to carry a mountain of

Tip...

Smart Tip

A line sheet should include simple line sketches of your products (both front and back), fabric information, style numbers, a list of colors each item comes in, and the wholesale price. You don't need to create expensive color line sheets—black-and-white sheets are perfectly fine, especially since you'll need new ones for each new collection.

▲

Bright Idea

Exhibiting at trade shows helps you build a strong reputation in your field. "You'll see the same buyers over and over, so you get to know them by sight, and you'll know what price point they're looking for," says Brooke Sobel, the San Francisco handbag designer. "Building relationships is really important in this business."

handbags with you to each appointment. Finally, you'll want to show the buyer a fabric and color sheet that has a swatch of each fabric used in the bags. This is so the buyer can touch and feel the hand of the fabric (i.e., the quality of the fabric based on how it feels to the touch).

After all these machinations, the hope is that the buyer will be so overcome with awe and delight that she will buy bags for the store she represents. However, be aware that depending on the store, "bags" could mean two or three. Still, it's a start, and one day you, too, could be selling 10,000 bags to Nordstrom as Brooke Sobel, the San Francisco handbag designer, has done.

Another way you can sell to retail buyers is to exhibit in a fashion accessories trade show. You'll find more information about this in Chapter 10, but for now, it's enough to know that the idea is to set up a display of your handbags at industry shows, then chat up every buyer who so much as looks your way. You'll also pass out line sheets and brave, hopeful smiles. If you come away with an order from a buyer at your first show, that's considered a good day. Any more orders than that and you're entitled to do a little Snoopy dance in the convention show atrium—you earned it!

Competition

The fashion industry may always be on the lookout for new and innovative handbag designers, but you will have to work hard to bring yourself and your collection to the attention of the media and retail buyers because there's so much competition. To begin with, your main competitors will be department stores like the Nieman Marcuses, Macy's and Kohl's of the world, as well as small boutiques, all of which are favorite haunts of women on a mission to buy new handbags. Virtual stores are also

Bright Idea

Because editors like to know the background behind a collection (it sparks ideas for articles), include an extra sheet in your press kit that explains your rationale behind the collection and where your inspiration came from. A paragraph or two is all you need to pique their interest.

strong competition—just check out BagBorrowandSteal.com, Zappos.com, and Shoes.com, all of which carry designer handbags, to see what we mean. The home shopping channels, including QVC and HSN, also have jumped on the fashion handbag bandwagon.

The good news is all these competitors can become your wholesale customers, too. You'll find out how to make that happen in Chapter 10.

Setting Prices

The price you set depends on whether you're selling wholesale or retail. The wholesale price should reflect the cost of the materials, labor, and markup (or

Bright Idea
Use hang tags on each item in your inventory to record information like the name of the handbag, its style number and its wholesale price. Use a different color each season so you can identify items in each collection at a glance.

profit). Typically the price will include a markup of 25 to 50 percent, a percentage that may vary depending on the final price point of the merchandise. For example, a more desirable item, like a high-end designer handbag, can sustain a higher markup because people are willing to pay more for the name and quality. On the other hand, a wool scarf would probably have a lower markup because the final retail price of such an item is much more modest.

Here's the basic formula for setting retail prices:

$$\text{Cost of goods} + \text{markup} = \text{retail price}$$

Typically, markup in the fashion industry is either "keystone" 100 percent markup—or a factor of 2.3 times. For example, the retail price on a bag that cost $100 wholesale would be $200 or $230, depending on the markup you use. You have to be careful about markup, however. As you know, things go on sale at the end of the season, which means that if you have to slash prices to move merchandise, you'll be cutting into your profit margin. That might be fine on occasions when you have a product that's a real barker (yes, it happens even to brilliant handbag designers) and you need to do anything necessary to move it out. But otherwise, you might have to increase the markup somewhat if you want to have a prayer of making a few bucks for your hard work.

Startup Costs

Depending on how you decide to structure your business, you could start your handbag empire on a shoestring—or on a Mt. Everest of cash. Starting as a home-based entrepreneur and crafting your own bags is the easiest and most affordable way to go. Hiring people to help with production on a one-by-one basis is fairly affordable, too, if you use fashion school students or other contract sewers. The most expensive option, of course, is manufacturing your product. That could cost you well into the six-figure range, so it's not a decision to be taken lightly.

▲

Case in point: One handbag designer we know of sank $300,000 into her startup, part of which was financed with funds from another successful business. While the handbag venture was successful, she ended up selling an 80 percent stake in the business because she didn't have the cash flow needed to meet the extremely large "dream" orders she received from a couple of prominent upscale retailers. "My choices were to go bankrupt, invest in the business, or go out of business," she says. "[At some point,] you can't do it all on your own because you have to put out so much money on leather and labor. My partner not only had the money but the business mind to make everything work, and now we not only fulfill orders, but we are working on a private label as well."

Brooke Sobel, the San Francisco handbag designer who made the switch from jewelry to purses, says expenses are never far from the mind of a handbag designer. "Think of it this way," she says. "Making jewelry equals pennies. Making bags equals $100 bills. Labor is more expensive, plus you learn the hard way not to pick the top leather, even if you want to as a way to get your name out. Probably 50 percent of my early bag costs were for materials and labor, which was scary."

To give you an idea of the costs associated with starting a handbag business, we've included a chart on page 37 detailing the sample startup costs for two fictitious businesses. Le Bel Sac (French for "Beautiful Handbag") is a homebased handbag design/build company with one employee (the owner) who is assisted by a pair of eager fashion design students who earn minimum wage. Pamplemousse, is a high-end handbag design company that manufactures its bags abroad. It, too, is homebased, but you'll see that its manufacturing costs are quite scary when viewed in the light of day. After you've reviewed these figures, take a shot at estimating your own startup costs using the worksheet on page 38.

Startup Expenses: Handbag Business

Item	Le Bel Sac	Pamplemousse
Mortgage/rent (first six months)		$3,600
Leasehold improvements ($10 to $15 per square foot; 600-square-foot space)		$6,000
Office equipment, furniture, supplies	$1,845	$6,152
Cut and sew tools, fabrics, supplies, packaging	$600	$1,200
Industrial sewing machine*		$1,000
Serger		$1,400
Manufacturing costs (first six months)		$24,000
Business licenses (estimated)	$100	$100
Phone (line installation charges)	$40	$150
P.O. box (first six months)	$54	$54
Employee wages, taxes, benefits (first six months)		$9,025
10 events x $100 per event		
Startup advertising (3% of projected revenue; first six months)	$200	$1,440
Legal services (startup package)		$900
Accounting services**		$500
Vehicle (sales calls transportation costs; first six months)	$1,200	$1,200
Travel (first six months)		$1,500
Insurance (annual cost)	$500	$500
Market research	$250	$500
Membership dues		$510
Publications (annual subscriptions) and books	$50	$100
Online service (broadband)	$99	$99
Website design	$1,000	$2,000
Web hosting, domain name	$10	$10
Subtotal	$5,948	$61,940
Miscellaneous expenses (roughly 10% of subtotal)	$600	$6,200
Total	**$6,548**	**$68,140**

*The low-end business starts out with a standard home sewing machine to keep costs low.
**The low-end business uses QuickBooks to keep track of expenses; the high-end business uses an accountant to set up the books.

Startup Expenses Worksheet

Item	
Mortgage/rent (first six months)	$
Leasehold improvements	$
Office equipment, furniture, supplies	$
Cut and sew tools, fabrics, supplies, packaging	$
Industrial sewing machine	$
Serger	$
Manufacturing costs (first six months)	$
Business licenses	$
Phone (line installation charges)	$
P.O. box (first six months)	$
Employee wages, taxes, benefits (first six months)	$
Startup advertising (3% of projected revenue; first six months)	$
Legal services	$
Accounting services	$
Vehicle (sales calls transportation costs; first six months)	$
Travel (first six months)	$
Insurance (annual cost)	$
Market research	$
Membership dues	$
Publications (annual subscriptions) and books	$
Online service (broadband)	$
Website design	$
Web hosting, domain name	$
Subtotal	$
Miscellaneous expenses (roughly 10% of subtotal)	$
Total	**$**

Belt, Scarf, and Hat Businesses

If ever there was ever an optimal time to start a belt, scarf, or hat business—or any combination thereof—this would definitely be it. According to the NPD Group, a global provider of consumer and retail market research information, women spent $2.6 billion on hats and scarves in a recent year, which represented an 11 percent increase in the category over the previous year. Driven by this escalating interest in accessories, top fashion designers featured chapeaux from the sublime to the ridiculous in their 2008 fall collections. Sarah Jessica Parker, aka Carrie Bradshaw, drew raves (and some derisive huzzahs) at the London premiere of *Sex and the City* by pairing a gorgeous green Alexander McQueen dress with a towering Phillip Treacy hat with embellishments that looked like they were plucked from an English garden. A young attorney and mom who were desperate for a funky belt to wear with jeans while *enceinte* launched a new line of fabric belts that now grace the closely watched waists of celebs like Kate Walsh and Jessica Alba. Celebrity knit scarves for breast cancer research and oversize "warm weather scarves" by Tolani Missoni worn knotted at the neck in place of a necklace are all the rage.

It's hard to say exactly why accessories have made such resurgence. Perhaps it's because of the sagging economy, which makes accessorizing, rather than buying a new wardrobe, very attractive to consumers. Maybe it's because it's possible to express your individuality and get a lot of look for the buck by accessorizing. Or maybe it's simply because accessorizing is the easiest way to update your look.

But what really matters is that now is a great time to cash in on today's accessories craze. This chapter will cover business information specific to belt, scarf, and hat designers. Now, we do realize that you may be interested in starting a wholesale business selling accessories to retailers and consumers without actually designing and manufacturing them yourself. If that's the case, you might find the startup information in subsequent chapters more useful for putting you on the path to accessories stardom. Feel free to go on ahead and we'll catch up with you later.

A Day in the Life

Like the other businesses discussed in this book, a belt, scarf, or hat business doesn't run on designing alone, no matter how brilliant those designs are. The owner of a small fashion accessories business handles any and every administrative task that comes down the pike, from office management to sales. In fact, the typical tasks you can expect to do on a daily or regular basis include:

- *Running the front office.* Opening the mail, answering e-mail and the phone.
- *Marketing and advertising.* To keep your business squarely in the public eye.
- *Locating suppliers, ordering materials and supplies.* This includes everything from yarn and other materials needed to make the accessories to office supplies like toner and copy paper. The internet is a great tool for locating suppliers, but if you're lucky enough to live close to one of the country's garment districts, you should start your fact-finding mission there.
- *Photographing accessories and writing product descriptions.* In addition to downloading descriptions and photos to your online store, you'll need this information

for your product line sheets, which are one-page sales sheets that you'll give to prospective retail customers (more on these in Chapter 13). Product photography is best left to professionals, but not every startup business owner can afford that. So invest in a digital camera that has a macro lens as well as a tripod to keep the camera steady, and start snapping away.

Unless you have absolutely no imagination (which is unlikely if you want to be an accessories designer), you should write the descriptions yourself. While clever and descriptive copy is great, a few sentences that give details like size or length, materials used, and product number will be sufficient.

- *Processing internet orders for a virtual store.* Includes processing credit card orders, packaging products, and shipping them out.
- *Performing website maintenance.* A must even if you don't have a lot of computer experience since it's unlikely that, as a fledgling entrepreneur, you'll be able to have your own computer expert on staff to do all this for you.
- *Running a retail store.* As mentioned previously, we recommend that you start your business as a homebased operation, then sell online. But if you intend to open a brick-and-mortar location, you'll have to staff the store, supervise any employees you may hire, manage inventory, restock shelves, meet with salespeople who want you to carry their products, oversee loss prevention, and so on.

Types of Products

Belts, scarves, and hats come in many shapes, styles, and sizes. Here's a look at the various types of accessories you can choose to sell:

Belts

Considering the close-fitting silhouette of today's fashions, it's clear that belts aren't being used to cinch garments for a slender look—rather, they're purely decorative. They often sit at the hip (what one fashion designer called "the new waist"), and they're meant to provide a counterpoint—often in bold and clashing terms—with the rest of a fashionista's attire.

The basic types of belts include:

- *Cummerbund.* Worn by men with formalwear, it's usually quite wide, often pleated, and usually coordinates with a bow tie.

- *Elastic.* At first glance, these belts may not seem to be the height of high fashion, but there is a segment of the population that buys them (weekend golfers come to mind). And when you consider that Prada has an elastic belt in its collection (retail price $172), there's good reason for you to consider designing them, too.

- *Fashion.* Made of fabric, canvas, webbing, ribbon, rope, nylon, leather, suede, exotic skins (i.e., crocodile) and vinyl, these belts are worn purely for decoration.

- *Ring sash.* This is a type of fabric (usually) belt that has a pair of rings on one end rather than a buckle, through which the fabric can be threaded and knotted

Virtually any other material can be used as a belt from ostrich feathers (a recent Prada look) to glass beads and recycled materials strung on leather thongs.

> **Fun Fact**
>
> Kerry Leikus, a former lawyer, burst on to the fashion accessories scene in late 2007 and single-handedly has made belts the new "it" accessory with her line of "Keggy" belts. The designer uses colorful retro woven and silk fabrics, and buckles in faux tortoise and pewter. These beautiful belts retail for $98 and up—definitely a nice chunk of change.

> **Fun Fact**
>
> The world's most famous silk scarf, created by French designer Hermès, debuted in 1937. There have been 25,000 Hermès scarf designs since then, each one made of 20mm silk. The company can produce 40,000 scarves in a week, each of which has a hand-rolled hem that takes 40 minutes to sew.

Scarves

There are many styles of scarves, including decorative lengths that can be knotted around the throat or at the waist, as well as mufflers, stoles, shawls, capes and wraps, and sarongs. Scarves come in woven fabrics and knits, in everything from luxurious natural fibers like cashmere and silk to fine wools like pashmina. Velvet, satin, silk georgette, chenille, rayon, and even manmade fibers like polyester are also used to make scarves in gorgeous hues.

While it's possible to buy an inexpensive knitted or crocheted scarf in any discount store, there are very high-end wool and silk yarns that can be used to create stunning, one-of-a-kind neckwear, knitted or crocheted either by hand or by machine. If you're planning to design knitwear, this is the quality of product you should aspire to carry in your own collection.

Hats

After a long hiatus, hats are suddenly hip again. Over the past few years, Coach has been leading the way with a signature monogrammed bucket hat, while Hollywood's young trendsetters have made trilbys and fedoras über-stylish for so-called "boyfriend dressing." Some of today's most popular fashion looks include:

- *Baseball cap.* A perennial favorite, now updated with the addition of cool embellishments.

- *Beret.* Flat cap most often worn in the winter and made of warm materials like wool or cashmere.

- *Boonie.* Wide-brimmed hat similar to a bucket hat but with a stiffer brim.

- *Bucket hat.* Floppy hat most often worn to keep the sun out of your eyes and off your face.

- *Cowboy hat.* Not just for those who ride the range, these hats are city chic. They come in a multitude of colors and are often embellished with leather cord, sequins, crystals, and shells.

- *Fedora.* A hat with a high, tapered crown. Two of the most famous fedoras in recent history were Humphrey Bogart's banded hat in *Casablanca*, and Harrison Ford's battered topper sported by his alter ego, *Indiana Jones*. Now young Hollywood has adopted the look.

- *Kentucky Derby hats.* There's no other term for these high-fashion chapeaux, which are traditionally worn to the famous race of the same name by society's most fashionable women. These magnificent hats usually have large brims and embellishments like silk hatbands and feathers. (Back in the day, designers actually perched whole birds' nests and their stuffed feathered occupants right on the brim!) These hats often are custom designed rather than mass produced so no two ladies need worry that someone else will steal their fashion thunder.

- *Newsboy cap.* A round, puffy hat with a fairly deep brim that's usually topped with a button.

- *Panama.* A wide-brimmed straw hat that's made a big comeback.

- *Toque.* The classic knit hat designed to ward off winter's chill.

- *Trilby.* Dapper hat similar to a fedora, but with a narrower brim.

- *Turban and miniturban.* In Western fashion, a hat made of a single piece of fabric wound around an inner cap.

Naturally there are many other types of hats and headwear, including headbands and visors, but those discussed above are the types you're most likely to design and/or manufacture for your hat business.

Tools and Supplies

If you choose to handcraft any of the accessories discussed in this chapter, you'll need:

- *Awl and/or leather punch.* For punching holes in leather belts.
- *Belt backing.* A stiffening product made of polypropylene that's used to make covered belts.
- *Belt buckle.* The finishing touch on a handcrafted belt.
- *Belt rings.* Pair of rings used to close a belt.
- *Fabric.* In various hues, textures, and weights. Naturally, silk is a great choice for scarves, while hats usually require sturdier fabrics like wool, cotton duck, felt, straw, leather, and so on. Belts can be made of virtually any material, as discussed earlier.
- *Industrial sewing machine.* For high-volume, high-speed, professional sewing.
- *Interfacing.* A type of fabric placed between a garment or accessory and the lining or facing to give an item shape or stability.
- *Knitting and crochet needles.* Metal or plastic, in various sizes.
- *Miscellaneous sewing tools.* Cutting board, dressmaker's shears, pinking shears, seam ripper, measuring tools, marking tools, pins, etc.
- *Ribbon.* Grosgrain or satin for amazing belts.
- *Serger (aka overcast machine).* For putting a decorative locked stitch on the edge of seams, as well as to prevent raveling of the fabric.
- *Stiffening.* For shaping a hat's crown or band.
- *Thread.* All-purpose, silk or embroidery.
- *Yarn.* For handcrafted scarves and hats.

Manufacturing Your Products

We really don't expect you to jump into manufacturing right at the start of your small-business career. Manufacturing is time-consuming and expensive. You'll have to spend a lot of time seeking a factory, either domestic or foreign, that's a suitable match for your product, then you may have to travel to the factory periodically to meet with manufacturing personnel. You'll also have much more paperwork related to expenditures, purchasing, materials (which have to be shipped to your manufacturer), shipping. You get the idea. It's a really big job for a startup business owner, so it's recommended that you avoid it at this stage. However, if you decide to manufacture

Silken Strands

Silk is wonderfully versatile for making fashion items of all types. Here's a rundown of the types of silk you'll encounter when searching for fabric for your designs:

- O *Chiffon.* The sheerest possible type of silk; generally requires a lining unless it's used for scarves.
- O *China silk.* A sheer, lightweight silk; also known as *habutai*, which means "soft and downy" in Japanese.
- O *Crepe de chine.* Very lightweight with a pebbled surface and a matte (non-reflective) finish; also known as CDC. Since it's wrinkle-resistant, it's most often used for apparel, but it's also suitable for scarves.
- O *Charmeuse.* A smooth, slinky fabric with a flat crepe backing and a shimmery satin front; its lustrous shine and luxurious feel make it a favorite of designers.
- O *Douppioni.* A plain weave silk with slubs, which are soft bumps in the silk yarn. These imperfections are not considered such by true silk aficionados since they add to the beauty of the fabric.
- O *Georgette.* A lightweight fabric similar to CDC, which has a grainy texture and drapes beautifully, making it perfect for apparel designers.
- O *Jacquard.* A fabric with an intricately woven pattern similar to brocade, which uses both matte and reflective threads.
- O *Noil.* Fabric made from the short fibers left over after combing and carding silk; looks like cotton but is wrinkle-resistant.
- O *Raw silk.* Untreated silk straight from the cocoon. Because natural "gum" that protects the fiber in the cocoon, known as sericin, remains on the fiber, fabric woven from it tends to be stiff and have a dull finish.
- O *Shantung.* A fabric with a firm, semi-crisp hand and a rough, nubby surface.
- O *Tussah.* Fabric made of short, coarse fibers; usually found in its natural shade of creamy tan.

goods, you absolutely should find a contract manufacturer rather than trying to set up your own facility. Tooling and other development costs are sky-high, so even if you have a big startup budget, it's insane to go that route. Instead, find a contract manufacturer, which, as the name implies, produces your accessories to specifications and leaves you out of that loop entirely. Trust us—it's the best way to go.

Selling Your Signature Fashion Goodies

Once your collection is designed and you have samples, you'll have to hit the road to sell it. This means calling on retailers who might be interested in carrying your products, like boutiques, gift shops, and department stores. Even the big chains may be on your hit list, although you must have sufficient production capability to play on the big boys' field of dreams, so for now you probably should concentrate on small chains instead. Start in your local market first to keep your travel costs down, then eventually widen your circle of influence as a way to grow your list of retail customers.

By the way, it helps to have a gift of gab to be an effective salesperson, but anyone can do it. "I just walked into a store and found out that no one bit me or kicked me out," says David Kulaas, the Golden, Colorado, designer of wildflower-inspired silk satin scarves. "I do get a lot of rejections, though."

Another viable outlet for selling your goods to retail buyers is through a fashion accessories trade show. You'll find more information about how to pull this off in Chapter 10, but basically it entails displaying your belts, scarves, and hats at industry shows, then working hard to convince buyers who pass by that they must have your accessories or die. The goal at such shows is to become a known player on the fashion accessories scene, as well as to scoop up as many orders as possible from retailer buyers.

Don't be too disappointed if you don't score big your first time out—frankly, there's a lot of competition for buyers' attention at trade shows. Still, trade shows are a good place to see and be seen, so you should do a few to get a feel for the industry.

Donna von Hoesslin, the Ventura, California, belt and jewelry designer, had limited success with the trade shows she's done in the past, but at least it was mostly due to logistics. "I was next to the men's section, which wasn't a great place to be if you're selling women's belts and jewelry," she says.

As a new exhibitor, you may not have much control over where your booth is placed. But it never hurts to try to negotiate a good location when you sign up.

Competition

Those very same boutiques, gift shops, and department stores you'll count among your prospective customers will be your competitors, too, because they'll be actively selling other designers' products. Other significant competitors include virtual stores, which have the reach of the entire web, as well as the other sellers at street fairs and craft shows where you decide to exhibit your accessories.

Of course, you'll have the same tools at your disposal as they do to promote your merchandise. The trick is to do what they do faster, better, and smarter. You'll find out how to do that in the coming chapters.

It's a Wrap

Here are what *Accessories* magazine predicts will be the newest trends in fashion scarves and wraps:

- Modern art and geometric prints
- Metallic threads and sequins
- Pleated gauze and open weaves
- Crochet knits
- Smocking and gathers
- Knife-pleated bias-cut oblongs
- Lace and ribbon borders
- Hand-knotted fringe
- Oversized bows
- Long, skinny neckties
- Silk charmeuse
- Neck tubes and cowls
- Cropped shrugs

Source: accessoriesmagazine.com

Setting Prices

This can be one of the trickiest tasks for a new business owner. Your prices have to be at the right level for the market, yet must allow you to recoup your material and labor costs and make a profit. The easiest way to calculate prices is by using cost pricing. Here's the basic formula:

Cost of goods + markup = retail price

The typical markup in the fashion industry is known as "keystone," which is a markup of 100 percent, although a markup of 2.3 times is also quite common in the apparel and related industries. Here's an example of how that would work on a belt that costs $50 to produce:

$50 wholesale price x keystone = $100 retail

or

$50 wholesale price x 2.3 = $115 retail

However, the pricing strategy you select absolutely must reflect what the market will bear. While you could be the next accessories superstar, which means you can write your own (sales) ticket, it's more likely that you'll have to be cognizant of what others are charging for similar accessories, because as Kulaas says, "You can't change spots on a leopard—customers set the demand."

So here's an example of how to make the cost/price equation work. Let's say you've produced a fabulous scarf that should retail at $75 to cover your costs. But your research shows that the most expensive scarf sold by the local department store is priced at $50. You'll have to scale back your product costs, perhaps by choosing a lesser quality silk or by using another material altogether, to make sure your costs are $25 or less so you can get a keystone markup on that scarf.

Checking out the competition before pricing merchandise is known as using competitive pricing. Competitive pricing doesn't take costs into account when setting the price—it only looks at what the competition is charging. However, at the end of the day your materials costs are an important part of the equation, so you'll have to contain them if you want to have any chance at making a profit.

Startup Expenses

Because the materials used to produce belts, scarves, and hats tend to be less expensive than the materials used by jewelry and handbag designers, you should be able to start your fashion empire pretty affordably. For example, von Hoesslin covered the launch of her belt and jewelry business out of savings, spending about $10,000 to $15,000 to design and develop an accessories line, travel to Bali to scout out factories, manufacture the products abroad, and set up a home office. Kulaas did it even more affordably. His stake of just a few thousand dollars covered a computer, the cost to ship samples back and forth to China, and a startup inventory of about $1,500 wholesale.

To help you estimate your own startup costs, we've included sample startup expenses for a couple of fictitious accessories companies on page 50. Velvet Topper, a homebased company that specializes in hats and scarves hand-knitted out of high-end, exquisite yarns, has the lower startup expenses, while That's a Wrap is a homebased belt and scarf company whose products are manufactured in Asia. The owner of this business also has a part-time employee who assists with office administration (since some of the owner's time is spent overseas), as well as with packaging and shipping.

Once you've had a chance to review the typical expenses incurred by these types of businesses and you've done some research of your own, try estimating your own expenses using the worksheet you'll find on page 51.

▲

Startup Expenses: Scarf, Belt, and Hat Businesses

Item	Velvet Topper	That's a Wrap
Mortgage/rent (first six months)		
Leasehold improvements ($10 to $15 per square foot)		
Office equipment, furniture, supplies	$1,845	$6,152
Yarn, supplies, packaging	$600	
Manufacturing costs (first six months)		$24,000
Business licenses (estimated)	$100	$100
Phone (line installation charges)	$40	$150
P.O. box (first six months)	$54	$54
Employee wages, taxes, benefits (first six months)		$4,500
10 events x $100 per event		
Startup advertising (3% of projected revenue; first six months)	$200	$1,440
Legal services (startup package)		$900
Accounting services*		$500
Vehicle (sales calls transportation costs; first six months)	$1,200	$1,200
Travel (first six months)		$1,500
Insurance (annual cost)	$500	$500
Market research	$250	$500
Membership dues		$510
Publications (annual subscriptions) and books	$50	$100
Online service (broadband)	$99	$99
Website design	$1,000	$2,000
Web hosting, domain name	$10	$10
Subtotal	$5,948	$44,215
Miscellaneous expenses (roughly 10% of subtotal)	$600	$4,400
Total	$6,548	$48,615

*The low-end business uses QuickBooks to keep track of expenses; the high-end business uses an accountant to set up the books.

Startup Expenses Worksheet

Item	
Mortgage/rent (first six months)	$
Leasehold improvements	$
Office equipment, furniture, supplies	$
Yarn, supplies, packaging	$
Manufacturing costs (first six months)	$
Business licenses	$
Phone (line installation charges)	$
P.O. box (first six months)	$
Employee wages, taxes, benefits (first six months)	$
Startup advertising (3% of projected revenue; first six months)	$
Legal services	$
Accounting services	$
Vehicle (sales calls transportation costs; first six months)	$
Travel (first six months)	$
Insurance (annual cost)	$
Market research	$
Membership dues	$
Publications (annual subscriptions) and books	$
Online service (broadband)	$
Website design	$
Web hosting, domain name	$
Subtotal	$
Miscellaneous expenses (roughly 10% of subtotal)	$
Total	$

To Market, to Market

U p to this point you've read about the business life of a fashion accessories business owner and the wide vistas of opportunity that exist. Now it's time to get serious about your prospects for success, something that you can determine by doing some rudimentary market research.

This is a step that many fledgling entrepreneurs skip in the excitement of establishing a business they love. But enthusiasm isn't enough. Unless you know who is primed and ready to buy from you, you can make some serious missteps that can literally put your business and ultimately your livelihood at risk. And, by the way, there's a need for market research no matter what type of business you're starting—wholesale, retail, or online. In every case you'll have money tied up in inventory, and if you're not reaching the right market, or if the market is soft because of recessionary times or because what you're selling is on the cusp of being passé, your inventory will languish and your bottom line will suffer.

Fortunately, you don't have to hire a high-priced marketer to help you plumb the mysteries of your market. "You can pretty much handle all the research by yourself on a reasonably small budget," says David Williams, associate professor of marketing in the School of Business Administration at Wayne State University in Detroit. "The problem is, many small-business owners view market research as an optional expense. But it's the only accurate way you have to find out what's important to your customer."

Here's how to determine what's important to fashion accessories customers.

Defining Your Audience

It might seem like a no-brainer—half the people in the world are women, and women love looking at and buying clothes, if the crowds at the mall are any indication. Since the well-dressed woman needs accessories to go with the skirts and blazers and other types of apparel they buy, it should follow that there's an automatic market for whatever fashion accessory you want to sell.

You hope. This is exactly the kind of wishful, rather misguided thinking that can get you into trouble. Big trouble. Here's an example: Lariat necklaces were hugely popular a couple of seasons ago. But if you watch the soaps (always a hotbed of up-to-date fashion trends), you'll see that the soap stars are wearing chunky silver necklaces with huge links. Or look up "lariat necklace" on qvc.com, and you'll find just 14 styles when once there were dozens. So now would not be the time to invest a lot of startup funds in lariat necklaces, no matter how good a deal you can cut with the wholesaler or how cute the merchandise is—to you, anyway.

So how do you figure out what people are buying? It really is as easy as keeping an eye on the media and doing your own internet research. Good sources of low-to-no-cost data

Beware!
Keep in mind that only a small segment of the fashion-buying public will buy an extremely expensive, exclusive brand of accessories. The reason is simple: Research shows that young women are the main purchasers of fashion and accessories, and they may not have the big bucks to spend on those hip and pricey products.

include the U.S. Census Bureau (for buying trends), fashion industry associations, trade and consumer publications, trade shows, and even the local library. And don't overlook the benefits of showing sketches of your designs or pictures of items you'd like to sell to friends, acquaintance and family members. (Tread lightly with the family's opinions—they love you no matter what you do, so they're not always the best source of objective advice.)

To determine the size of your market and the pool of prospective buyers, start by looking at industry statistics. You'll find some pertinent figures in Chapter 1 of this book, as well as other valuable information from sources like

Beware!
Never try to manufacture or even purchase wholesale accessories en masse before you figure out who will actually buy them from you. You must have a legitimate market for everything you sell or you'll be left holding the bag ... or the necklace ... or whatever else you choose to sell. So do your market research well.

the national press (*The Wall Street Journal*, *The New York Times*), organizations like the Accessories Council (accessoriescouncil.org), and fashion industry bibles like *Women's Wear Daily*. The logical market to focus on is women's accessories since products for women make up such a substantial percentage of the fashion accessories market, but it's also possible to sell men's accessories successfully, as Atlanta entrepreneurs Reagan Hardy and Emmie Howard do. Not to mention men's accessories don't change radically from season to season, so you might even have a little edge in the sales wars if you cater to the men's furnishings market.

Not all your market research will be based on informed guesswork. Naturally seasonality is a determinant of success (think pashmina scarves in the winter and floaty silk creations in the spring and summer). So is location. You're not likely to sell a lot of high-end Gucci handbags in a college town, but fun costume jewelry is probably a sure bet. In fact, it's usually a good idea to approach those very high-end accessories with caution. The segment of the fashion market that can afford them is actually quite small relative to the rest of the population. Those customers are usually "socialites," career or older women who have higher disposable incomes, while the fashion enthusiasts among us tend to be younger and hipper. Since the terminally hip tend to be more interested in fashion and quantity rather than quality, it makes more sense for the fledgling accessories business owner to cater to them and leave the really high-end merchandise to the couture designers.

Location, Location, Location

Speaking of college towns and gated communities, if you're planning to open a retail location, you have to be very aware of the demographics of the community in which you'll open your doors. Demographics are the characteristics of the people in

▲

your target audience that make them more likely to buy your products or use your services. Among these characteristics are age, education, income level, gender, type of residence, and geographic location. The importance of age and gender is obvious—as mentioned previously, young women tend to be the most enthusiastic consumers of fashion accessories. Geographic location (as in West Coast vs. New England, or the Midwest vs. the South) can also impact consumer behavior. For instance, you're probably a lot more likely to see hats in the Northeast (where the winters are long and frigid) or in the South, where events like the Kentucky Derby are a boon for the local chapeau economy.

What the other categories, including education, income level, and type of residence, have in common is disposable income. Presumably people who are better educated (i.e., professional women) have higher paying jobs, while those with a higher income level and a more expensive homestead probably have more money to spend (or, perhaps more realistically, higher credit limits). So pay close attention to the local community to get a good indication of how much your neighbors might be willing to spend.

Finally, the economic climate is another indicator of future success. If there's a downturn in the economy and gas and food prices are on the rise, then a cute little fashion accessories shop on Main Street, right between a couple of boarded-up businesses, is *not* going to have much chance of success. Naturally, you can't predict the future, but if you observe that the local economy is heavily dependent on a particular industry—say, automobiles—then you probably don't want to locate your new business in that particular place because it doesn't take a fortuneteller to know that the industry will have its ups and downs. A better location might be in a mall that has a high occupancy rate or in a resort town where tourists are likely to stock up on souvenirs to take back home.

Conducting Market Research

A good way to determine what the market will bear is to do some research on the local economy. Your chamber of commerce and municipal economic development department usually have data like the percentage of people who are employed full time and the types of jobs they hold, while Census Bureau data (census.gov) can tell you the number of people by age range in the community. Other reliable sources of statistical information include state and federal agencies, which tend to collect data on

Showing Off

Every entrepreneur has grandiose visions of discovering the next "It" product that will make him or her famous—and rich. But the reality is, it takes a lot of work and time to build a loyal clientele, and most of the time, you have to start generating the buzz gradually at the grassroots level.

The obvious places to start marketing your fashion accessories include craft shows, street fairs, and other local events. You'll have plenty of opportunities at such venues to chat up anyone who wanders by, find out what they like or don't like about what's on the table, and get ideas about what else they might be interested in buying that you don't carry yet. This is primary research that's invaluable to a fledgling entrepreneur—and to your startup budget, for that matter, since it would cost a lot more to hire a market research firm to do the same kind of due diligence for you.

The other part of the market research equation is determining what other artisans are selling and how much they're charging to make sure your own products are in line. So when you do a show, bring a helper along so you can spend some time roaming around yourself. A word of caution, however: If you want to jot down your observations, do it discreetly. Designers are notoriously protective of their designs, so you don't want to appear to be making notes so you can knock off their designs later.

everything from income levels to buying habits; the SBA (sba.gov); and even utility companies, which generally will share the demographic data they gather at no charge or for a small administrative fee.

Don't overlook the internet as a source of secondary research. Just be selective about the material you access. As you know, anyone with 10 bucks can sign up for his or her own domain name and post virtually anything that comes to mind. Stick with the leading fashion industry sources when you're looking for information. You'll find a list of some reputable organizations to explore in the Appendix.

Speaking of the internet, when it comes to determining your market in cyberspace, all bets are off. According to apparel market demographics (information that was located on the internet, of course), nearly 7 million women shop online for fashions. When you consider that there are more than 300 million Americans, that might not sound like a very high percentage. But the point is, there's a pool of 7 million women out there who regularly surf the internet for fashion, and if you come to the attention of just a small percentage of them, you could find yourself with a substantial amount of business, and it really won't matter which income, age or other demographic group the sales come from. You'll find more information about how to use the internet as a marketing tool in Chapter 14.

Writing a Mission Statement

No discussion of market research would be complete without a nod to the mission statement, that tool used by big corporations and small ventures alike to describe the overall purpose of the business and suggest strategies for success. Since a mission statement is rather like a road map to success, even small businesses like yours should have one.

Smart Tip

Industry publications are a great source of market research background information. Try Googling "fashion publication" or a variation of that term to see what turns up, or head for your local library and page through the *Standard Rate and Data Service* directory (published by VNU), which lists tons of publications in every category known to man—or woman.

A mission statement should contain information like:

- A statement about whom you serve
- A description of your company's purpose and goals
- A few words about how you'll achieve those goals
- A timetable for achieving goals
- A forward-looking statement about what achieving those goals will mean to the business

Incidentally, it's not necessary to include all these points, as this mission statement from Claire's Stores, a well-known mall chain of fashion accessories stores, demonstrates:

> Our vision is to be the world's most popular brand for girls, young adults and women in search of costume jewelry, fashion accessories and other products that enhance their lifestyle.
>
> To attain that objective, our mission is to provide customers with an unparalleled selection of fashion and fun products at reasonable prices. Furthermore, within our stores, we strive to create an environment that is fun, welcoming, and that encourages customers to tap into their creativity and explore their personal styles.

As you can see from this example, a mission statement also helps to keep your business on track. If this chain's buyers were tempted to stock up on cute wedding attire for dogs, for example, it would only take a quick review of the mission statement to remember that dog duds don't fit the product mix. Adding them to the inventory could actually confuse the buyer about what products to expect in this chain's stores, and ultimately could affect the bottom line negatively.

The easiest way to write a mission statement is to determine the scope and size of your target market, then create the mission statement with that body of buyers in mind. Here are a few sample mission statements:

- Chloe's Cinchers takes belts to a new level of sophistication, with their supple leathers and skins and top-of-the-line hardware. They're perfect for women on the move beyond the glass ceiling of corporate America who want a polished yet stylish look.
- Jen's Jewels produces one-of-a-kind bracelets and rings of art-piece caliber that will be sold at medium-to-large art fairs and art galleries in metro San Francisco.
- Funky and fashionable are the watch words for In the Bag, a handbag design company that will use local artisans to design and stitch high-end, one-of-a-kind bags.

Finally, here's the actual mission statement for Southern Proper, the men's accessories business owned by Reagan Hardy and Emmie Howard:

Southern Proper is [the maker of] a line of neckties, clothing and accessories that portray the heritage and charm of the Southern United States. Our products express the roots and pride that consumers have for the South and its characteristics. Our products have a distinct style that Southern women have adored on men throughout the ages. These products give each man a 'Proper Southern Style' that will live on for generations to come.

"A company cannot truly be successful without a mission statement," Hardy stresses. "It provides the framework for a brand and helps to create a brand identity as well."

Try brainstorming your own mission statement using the worksheet on page 60.

Mission Statement Worksheet

To start the thought process toward creating a great mission statement, answer the following questions:

1. What are your reasons for becoming a fashion accessories retailer/wholesaler/designer?

    _____

    _____

2. What are your personal objectives? How do you intend to achieve them?

    _____

    _____

3. What skills do you bring to the business that will be benefit it?

    _____

    _____

4. What is your vision for this business? Where do you think you can take it in one, two, and five years?

    _____

    _____

Using this information, write your mission statement here:

Mission Statement for _____
(your company name)

_____

_____

_____

Fashioning Your Business

Designing and/or searching for amazing and creative accessories that everyone will clamor for is just part of the process of establishing your new business (and the most fun part, at that). But before you take the creative leap into those activities, you need to establish yourself as a legitimate business owner. So in this chapter, we'll touch on the various tasks you must do to lay the groundwork for a successful business launch, including selecting a corporate structure, choosing and registering your company name, addressing zoning and licensing issues, and writing one of the most important documents in your life—namely, your business plan.

Legal Lingo

One of the most important steps you must take at the dawn of your new business empire is to select a legal structure for your business. This serves several purposes. First, it sends a message to Uncle Sam that you're a serious businessperson, not just a kitchen table hobbyist. Second, it allows you to take certain tax write-offs that will help your bottom line. Finally, it helps to limit your personal liability, depending on which legal form you choose, which can be a lifesaver if some crazed customer or supplier decides to sue you for some unfathomable reason.

There are four types of for-profit legal structures. They include sole proprietorship, partnership, corporation, and limited liability corporation (LLC). Each has its own advantages and benefits; for now, here's a brief description of each form.

Sole Proprietorship

This is the easiest type of business to form, which is why it's the choice of many fashion-accessories business owners in their startup phase. Basically all you have to do is file for an assumed name (something we'll talk about a little later), then open a business checking account in that name. At tax time, you'll have to file Schedule C (Profit or Loss From Business) and Schedule SE (Self-Employment Tax) with your personal income taxes, and you'll have to pay estimated taxes on a quarterly schedule. But that's about it. On the negative side, as a sole proprietor you'll be personally responsible for any losses, bankruptcy claims, legal actions, and so on related to the business, claims that also can put your personal assets at risk.

Partnership

A partnership is great when it works well—and can be a nightmare when it doesn't. Assuming you pick the right partner(s), you'll find the formation of a partnership quick and easy because there aren't any documents to file. There also are a number of tax benefits with this type of legal structure. However, because each partner is responsible for the actions of the other, it's usually a good idea to have an attorney draw up articles of partnership so there are no misunderstandings between the partners concerning responsibilities, personal investment, and the many other issues that will crop up in the course of running the business. It also pays to have a termination or exit plan in case one partner wants out—or you want him or her out for the good of the company.

College friends Reagan Hardy and Emmie Howard, co-owners of Southern Proper in Atlanta, cite their long friendship and complementary skills for the success of their partnership. "We have different talents and personalities, as well as different core strengths," Hardy says. "When we started the business, we did everything together, from the paperwork to the decision making. But after a year, we defined our roles based on those core strengths, which for Emmie are operations, product development, and marketing; and for me are public relations and sales. It also helps that we have a great friendship and great family support."

But there's another strong reason why the pair work so well together. "We do a great job separating business and pleasure," Hardy says. "At the end of the day our friendship is more important than anything else."

Corporations

This type of business arrangement is established as a legal entity that's completely separate from the business owner, which means his or her personal assets are not at risk if the company experiences financial difficulties. There are two types of corporations: the S corporation and the C corporation. The S corporation is usually favored by small-business owners because it has many tax advantages—but at the same time it has a number of corporation-specific requirements, like annual meetings and a board of directors.

> ## Smart Tip
> **Tip...**
>
> Small-business owners who wish to incorporate are usually advised to form an S corporation because it blends the tax benefits of the sole proprietorship with the limited liability and prestige of a corporation.

While an attorney will happily handle the incorporation of your business, you actually can incorporate on your own for only about $150 to $450. (You can expect to pay $500 to $1,000 if an attorney does the deed.) However, since corporate law is complex and difficult to understand, you might just want to pony up the dough and let a professional handle the job.

Limited Liability Company

The final type of legal entity is the limited liability company, or LLC, which offers the advantageous tax structure of both partnerships and corporations while limiting the personal liability of the owner. The good news is you don't pay corporate taxes with an LLC. The bad news: You'll have a lot of the same reporting requirements as an S corporation, and you could run into additional requirements if you're planning to operate in more than one state (red alert—that includes if you sell virtually).

With this dizzying array of choices, how do you pick the best legal structure for your situation? Start by hiring an attorney who can give you good advice. "There are advantages to each kind of entity, and an attorney can help you decide which one is best for your situation," says Daniel H. Minkus, a member of the business practice group Clark Hill PLC in Birmingham, Michigan. "If you don't know the people you are doing business with, I'd encourage you to form a single-member LLC or corporation. They're simple to create, and they're invaluable because your clients are dealing with your enterprise and not with you personally."

Naming the Business

Choosing a name for your company is a lot like selecting a name for your child—you'll be living with it a long time, so it should be strong and memorable, as well as easy to pronounce and spell. However, in the fashion industry clever names abound and in some cases even lend an air of glamour or exclusivity to the brand. So if you want to choose something cutting edge, just be sure the name isn't too over the top because it will be difficult for your valued customers to remember. That is, unless some celebrity starts wearing/carrying/talking about your products—then you're golden, no matter what your name.

In fact, that's exactly what happened to Ruta Fox, the New York-based creator of the Ah Ring, a slender diamond band in white gold for single women who are "available" and "happy." The clever and meaningful name gave her a hook to market the pinkie ring, which ultimately came to the attention of talkmeister Oprah Winfrey's camp. After the ring was featured in *O The Oprah Magazine*, sales took off, resulting in first-year sales in the seven-figure range and an exciting new career for the then-unemployed copywriter.

Picking a clever name that's related to your target market is another viable option. Donna von Hoesslin, the California belt and jewelry designer, named her company "Betty Belts and Betty B." because "Beach Bettys" is slang in the surfing community for "surfer chicks," as she calls them. "It just worked out because of the alliteration," she says.

Reagan Hardy and Emmie Howard scored a similar regional hit with the name for their men's accessories company, Southern Proper. Before launching their brand, the partners surveyed more than 100 men who grew up in the South and asked them to list what things came

Smart Tip

You can find a list of the requirements and links to state offices for business name registration (aka "DBA") on the SBA's page at business.gov/guides/business-law/business-name/dba.html. The business.gov site also has a lot of other useful information for small-business owners, including a link to required permits by state.

Bright Idea

Clever and witty business names are fine, but make sure it's obvious from the name what type of business you're in. By the same token, don't select such a narrowly focused name that there's no room for future business expansion. For example, Bracelets by Julia dooms its namesake to sell bracelets forever—or to rename the business later.

to mind when they thought of the South. "A majority of the guys listed manners and saying, 'Yes, ma'am' and 'No, ma'am'," Hardy says. "Since being 'proper' was a huge part of the Southern lifestyle and because we wanted to incorporate the word 'Southern' into our brand, Emmie and I decided that 'Southern Proper' was a fitting name and wouldn't limit our brand if we decided to expand into other sectors, including women's clothing/accessories as well as dog accessories."

Classic and elegant names also do well in the fashion industry. Brooke Sobel, the San Francisco handbag designer, added a couple of letters to her own last name and—*voilà*—a high-end, European-sounding company name was born. In addition to having an exclusive ring to it, the name "Sobella" is a stylish corruption of "so beautiful" (*bella* is Italian for beautiful).

Of course it's also quite common in the fashion industry to name your company after yourself. (Think Kate Spade or Diane von Furstenberg.) However, since you don't have any name recognition when you're first starting out, you may want to save your name for a future product line that hopefully will morph out of your wildly successful first fashion accessories business.

Being the creative type you undoubtedly are, you may already have picked out the perfect, evocative name for your business. But if you need some help settling on just the right name, try brainstorming using the worksheet on page 70.

Make It Official

Of course, selecting the perfect moniker is just part of the naming process. Next, you have to register it as a fictitious company name (known as an assumed name, or DBA, for "doing business as"). Most states require businesses to register their name as a way to make sure it's unique, as well as to give the business owner the exclusive right to use it. (You can find a list of states and their assumed name requirements at business.gov/guides/business_law/dba.html.)

Depending on where you live, you may have to appear in person at the secretary of state, county, or parish government office, where you'll file a DBA statement. The fee is usually nominal. For instance, it's just $10 in Macomb Country, Michigan; $25 in Sacramento County, California; and $50 in the entire state of Oregon. This gives you the right to use the name for a limited period of time, usually three to five years, although some states like Idaho award DBAs in perpetuity. Then you simply renew it for as long as you need it.

Before you get your DBA, however, a search must be conducted to make sure your name is unique. Many states have online lists of business names that you can search yourself, or you may have to pay the government entity to handle the search for you. In any event, it's always possible that the name you've selected is already being used, so you should have a couple of names as backups just in case.

> **Bright Idea**
>
> Once you've selected a company name, consider applying for a registered trademark right away to protect your name as you build your brand. That will keep others from trying to latch onto your success by imitating it, plus a trademark actually adds value to your brand, especially if one day your products become widely known.

In the Zone

Starting a business out of your home is a cost-effective way to get the operation up and running. But some municipalities prohibit businesses from operating in residential neighborhoods because of the potential for excessive traffic and noise. So to make sure all is copasetic with your local government, check to see whether there are any zoning regulations that apply to home businesses. If you're planning to see customers in your home (unlikely) or will be bringing in a horde of people to help with packaging and shipping merchandise (more likely), your local government may have something to say about your operation. Sometimes all it takes is a good neighbor attitude and a zoning variance to placate the local suits.

Road Map to Success

The final thing you'll need before launching your business is a thoughtfully conceived and well-executed business plan that focuses on both short- and long-term goals. Toward that end, it should outline your plans, goals, and strategies for making your business successful. Its main purpose is to help steer your company through the high and low tides of business ownership, but it's an absolute necessity if you're planning to seek financing or attract investors.

While you can pay someone the big bucks to craft your first business plan, you really should do the deed yourself because, after all, you're the expert on what you expect to do with the business and how you'll get there. There are a number of resources on the internet that can help guide you through the process, including the

Licensed to Thrill

Most states require business owners—no matter whether their business is organized as a sole proprietorship, partnership, corporation or LLC—to have certain operating permits. This also includes the owners of home-based businesses.

The most common type of license is a business license, which is available from your local government. It's usually fairly inexpensive and renewable annually. In addition, every state requires retailers and wholesalers to have a seller's permit, which allows them to purchase ready-made goods and materials (like leather for handbags or beads for jewelry) for resale without paying tax. Depending on which state you're in, you may need a sales tax license in addition to or in lieu of a seller's permit, which also allows you to purchase materials and goods for resale without paying sales tax. The application process and fees vary by state, so check your state's website or phone your local government office to find out how to apply.

If you'll be producing accessories and selling them wholesale, you'll also need a wholesaler's license, which is usually available from your state's department of treasury or a similarly named department. Again, the cost varies by state.

Your state may have other licensing requirements. To find out whether you need any other special permits or licenses, or for help locating the right state agencies to which to apply, you can contact:

- ○ *SBA.* See the federal listings in your phone book, or go to sba.gov.
- ○ *SCORE: Counselors to America's Small Business.* Go to score.org. This non-profit organization is an SBA partner and has hundreds of chapters throughout the United States.
- ○ *Small Business Development Centers (SBDC).* Reachable through the SBA, or by logging onto sba.gov, then clicking on the "Local Resources" tab.

insight found on Entrepreneur's website at entrepreneur.com/businessplan. You'll also find additional insights you can trust from the SBA at sba.gov.

A successful business plan should have the following major components:

- *Executive summary.* This section summarizes the entire business plan and describes the company and products you'll offer. It also touches on the legal form of operation (discussed earlier in this chapter) and your goals. If you're planning to seek financing for your company, be sure to include details about your plans and strategies for growing the business in this section.

▲

- *Business description.* In addition to describing your business (i.e., manufacturing and marketing handbags, or designing and handcrafting high-end jewelry), you also should provide some details about the fashion industry in general and your target market in particular. As you may recall, there are some general statistics about the fashion industry in Chapter 1 that you can use as a starting point. One good source for information is your local Small Business Development Center. Go to sba.gov, then click on "Local Resources."

- *Market strategies.* Here's where you'll put the market research you gathered to good use as you outline the strategies you'll use to reach prospective customers, focusing on any statistics you have related to your target market (like, for instance, the number of women aged 18 to 25 who buy jewelry). Be sure to emphasize anything that makes your company unique, such as your personal history as a jewelry designer, for instance, or your knowledge of manufacturing processes gleaned from a previous career in another field.

- *Competitive analysis.* Using the potential competitors mentioned in each of the fashion business chapters of this book, consider what you'll do to make your business successful. Maybe the difference will be your price point (higher quality for a lower cost), exclusivity (available only in limited quantities), or exceptional detailing (unusual or innovative embellishments). Discuss how these differences make your product(s) new and exciting, which ups their desirability quotient. Be specific. Do you want to compete with Prada (couture bags) or Kate Spade (fun but affordable bags)? Once you figure out your niche, you can determine how to market your merchandise.

- *Design and development plan.* This section should focus on how you'll develop local market opportunities, as well as setting timetables for achieving them. For example, while you may start out by selling your custom-made jewelry in your own boutique, as California designer Liza Sonia Wallach does, your goal may be to get your designs into other high-end boutiques, too. Create a plan and a timetable for making that happen and include it in your business plan.

- *Operations and management plan.* Using the information found in Chapters 2 to 4 of this book, discuss the day-to-day operations of your business, as well as the background of the management team (that's you). You should also include financial details like cost of goods sold, capital requirements (if applicable), and

Startup Checklist

❑ Choose the appropriate legal form for the business.

❑ Select a business name (and a spare) and apply for an assumed name (aka DBA).

❑ File incorporation papers, if applicable, or find an attorney to assist.

❑ Check local zoning regulations pertaining to home businesses; request a zoning variance, if necessary.

❑ Apply for a business license.

❑ Write the business plan.

❑ Apply for financing, if necessary.

operating expense information. You'll learn how to create an income and expense chart that you can use in your business plan in Chapter 16.

• *Financial factors.* Even if you don't plan to take on investors or cast your lot with your local bank, you still need to forecast your expenses and potential profits as a way to gauge how successful you'll be. Toward that end, you should develop an income worksheet, balance sheet and cash flow statement. Go to entrepreneur.com for more information on how to develop these important tools.

That probably sounds like a lot of work and—honestly—it is if you've never written a business plan before. But even though you're probably more interested in creating fashion accessories than creating a business plan, don't neglect this important business-building step. You likely wouldn't set off on a cross-country trip without a map or a portable GPS device. You'll be just as rudderless when you set sail on your new business venture if you don't have a business plan to guide you.

▲

A Name Is Born

Although there are plenty of fashion businesses with funky or unusual names (think Juicy Couture), many more are simply named after the designer. So unless your name is John Smith or something most people would find completely unpronounceable, you might want to follow the lead of the industry's famed designers and turn your birth name into a brand name. (Although the name BCBGMAXAZRIA—the way it often appears even though it's supposed to be BCBG Max Azria—doesn't seem to have hurt designer Max Azria any.)

But there's no reason why you can't select a unique name like Southern Proper co-owners Reagan Hardy and Emmie Howard did. Try the following brainstorming exercise to come up with a name you'll love:

List the top three things that come to mind when you hear the word "fashion" (such as "stylish" or "trendy"):

1. _____

2. _____

3. _____

Consider how you'd like people to think or feel about your products. Write down those adjectives. Use a thesaurus to get a full range of choices. Also consider foreign translations of those words, like Brooke Sobel did when she created "Sobella."

1. _____

2. _____

3. _____

Think about how and where customers will wear or use your product. (With formalwear? On the beach? At a club?)

1. _____

2. _____

3. _____

A Name Is Born, continued

Now, try combining elements from these three sections in different ways:

1. _____

_____

2. _____

_____

3. _____

_____

Don't judge these possibilities yet. Try saying them out loud to make sure they're easily understood, both in person and over the phone. Still like them? Then put them to the test: Search the internet to check trademarks and domain names to make sure no one else in the fashion industry is using them. Then check with your local county seat to see if anyone has claimed them already. Hopefully at least one of the names on your list will survive all these checks—and a new company name will be born.

Calling in the
Professionals

Whether you've been casually selling fashion accessories as a little side business or you're starting a new operation from square one, chances are the main reason you're interested in having a business is because it's a creative outlet for your talents and because you enjoy having the freedom to do what you want. It's probably not because you love crunching numbers, agonizing over business taxes, troubleshooting computer problems, or handling myriad other operational duties. Yet these are all activities a small-business owner must undertake to keep the business running smoothly.

Or not. No one says you personally have to handle those tasks that 1) you're too busy to do; 2) you don't have a clue how to do; or 3) you passionately, profoundly hate doing. Instead, you can engage the services of a select group of professionals—specifically, an attorney, accountant, computer specialist, and insurance agent—to look out for your best interests and get some of those less desirable jobs off your fashion plate.

Now, we know your startup budget will probably be so tight it squeaks. But it truly is worth it to pass along those time-consuming and brain-numbing operational tasks to experienced professionals rather than trying to do everything yourself and finding the joy of running your own creative business dimming by the hour. Here are some tips on how to pick your professional posse.

Legal Liaison

If you've ever watched the wacky antics of attorneys on prime-time TV shows like *Boston Legal*, you might think that hiring an attorney would be absolutely at the bottom of your business wish list. But the truth is a lawyer is very valuable when it comes to protecting your company, personal assets, and intellectual property (i.e., any products you invent). He or she also can lend an ear (albeit an *expensive* one) when you have a problem and don't know where to turn.

Other reasons to hire an attorney include:

- You want to form a partnership or corporation.
- You're presented with a contract that is complex or difficult to understand.
- You're signing a contract for a lot of money or one that will cover a long period of time (such as a long-term manufacturing agreement or a lease for a retail site).
- You're being sued or someone is threatening to sue you.
- You need help with tax planning, loan negotiations or employee contracts.
- You wish to protect intellectual property.

But above all, an attorney can help you avoid expensive mistakes you might make if you try to go it alone.

Dollar Stretcher

Want the peace of mind that comes with having an attorney on your team but not the big price tag? Then try a prepaid legal plan. Prepaid plans usually offer a package of services, like unlimited phone consultations with an attorney, contract review, and discounts on other legal services at an affordable rate—sometimes as low as $10 a month.

Protecting Your Turf

You have a great idea for a new piece of jewelry, a rockin' handbag, or a fabulous belt. No one else is making anything remotely like it as far as you can tell. So should you be concerned someone will steal your idea and produce a similar product, especially if your product appears headed for the Accessory Hall of Fame? Absolutely, says David Cornwell, director at the intellectual property law firm Stern, Kessler, Goldstein, & Fox PLLC in Washington, DC. "Infringement is more and more of an issue today because once a product hits the shelves, it will be copied by competitors," he says. "The number of infringement cases has sky-rocketed in the last few years."

U.S. copyright law automatically protects your designs as soon as they're put on paper, created with a computer program, or made into a prototype. However, proving that you are the owner of such designs can be difficult. It's a good idea to file a U.S. copyright application or trademark your product, as New York jewelry retailer Ruta Fox did with her product, the Ah Ring. Neither process is difficult, but it can be expensive, and it's one area you might not want to navigate on your own, especially since you might have to pursue legal avenues to protect your work. For assistance, contact an attorney who specializes in intellectual property or trademark law and can advise you how to proceed or what to do if you find out that someone is knocking off your accessories.

You don't have to spend a fortune to obtain legal counsel. To begin with, many attorneys offer an initial consultation at no charge, which allows you to determine whether your personalities mesh well. You also can keep the cost down by hiring someone in a one- or two-person office rather than a high-priced attorney from a large firm. Some attorneys also offer small-business startup packages, which usually cover basic correspondence as well as incorporation and other startup activities and cost only about $500 to $900. Otherwise, attorneys' fees usually run about $100 to $450 an hour.

To find an attorney, ask business acquaintances for a referral, check with your state's attorney referral service, or check out the *Martindale-Hubbell Law Directory* at martindale.com.

Capital Help

If bookkeeping and other financial management tasks are not your favorite pastimes, then you definitely need to find a bookkeeper or an accountant to help manage your financials. Often a bookkeeper is sufficient to launch your financial kingdom. He or she will help you establish an effective record-keeping system, keep expenses in line, handle data entry and monitor cash flow—in short, oversee all financial recording aspects of the business. But if your business tax situation is complex, you have employees, your billings are complicated, or you need any kind of financial analysis or business planning, then you will need an accountant instead.

Because accountants are college educated and certified, their services cost more than those of a bookkeeper. According to a survey by Intuit, the highest rate for accountants who perform bookkeeping services is $71 an hour, while owners of small general bookkeeping firms charge an average of $49 an hour. In fact, the same survey showed that the low-end rate for general bookkeepers is just $10 to $20 an hour, which is certainly compatible with the budget of a startup fashion accessories business (especially since you'll probably only need a few hours of their time every month).

If you really want to save money when you start out and you feel confident enough to handle your own books, you can use one of the accounting software packages on the market. Intuit QuickBooks is the choice of many small-business owners because it's so easy to use and has many useful tools. For instance, you can create estimates, invoices and customized reports, as well as print checks, track expenses, and much more. You can download the Simple Start Free Edition at quickbooks.intuit.com. Keep in mind, though, that if you decide to do your own bookkeeping, you have to make time to do it—and that takes time away from your core business.

It's usually best to get a referral to an accountant or bookkeeper from your attorney, banker, or other business professionals whose judgment you respect. Alternatively, you can get a referral to a qualified practitioner by visiting the American Institute of Certified Public Accountants' website at aicpa.org. In any event, try to select someone who has experience with small-business clients, since he or she is more likely to be tuned into the tax, finance, and other issues you face as a small-business owner.

Super-Computer Consultant

If you've ever been baffled by the Blue Screen of Death or had a cyber gremlin scramble up your bits and bytes, then you probably don't have to be convinced that you need a computer specialist on your business management team. A computer consultant can tune up your hardware and software, delete unwanted programs or malicious code, and otherwise maintain your system so it's always running at peak capacity. This type of expert is also invaluable when something does go wrong with your computer while

> **Tip...**
>
> ### Smart Tip
> Even if you have a bookkeeper or accountant, it's crucial to maintain daily records of every financial transaction so you always know how the business stands. QuickBooks can help you keep track, or you can set up a simple spreadsheet in Excel to record debits and credits.

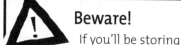

you're in the middle of processing the biggest order of your life, ordering pizza for all-nighter packaging parties, and so on.

Computer consultants generally charge by the hour (around $50 per hour is pretty common). Be sure to pick someone who makes house calls and guarantees his work. As with lawyers and accountants, it's usually best to ask around for a referral to a reputable computer consultant. If you live in a major urban area, you also can contact Best Buy's Geek Squad, which offers 24-hour in-home computer support. Call (800) GEEK SQUAD or visit geek-squad.com for a list of services and fees.

> **! Beware!**
> If you'll be storing expensive products or materials like gemstones, sterling silver or gold in your home, you'll need a valuable items floater for your homeowner's policy. Likewise, valuable items that are stored in a safe deposit box until you need them should have valuable article in-vault coverage since losses from safe deposit boxes are unlikely but not impossible.

The Great Protector

The final business professional you should have on your team is an insurance agent or broker. Insurance agents handle insurance products from a single company, while a broker is an independent agent who represents the products of many companies. As a result, a broker often can get you better rates. If you're interested in saving money (and who isn't), you could use one of those discount brokers on the internet. But it's usually a better idea to find an agent or broker in your community so you have someone to go to when you have questions or concerns—especially since you're likely to have a lot of questions about the best way to protect your personal and business assets.

If you're happy with the person who currently insures your home, apartment, or car, you may be able to work with them for your business insurance needs, too. However, not all companies are willing to insure homebased businesses, so either ask your current agent for a recommendation or look in the Yellow Pages under "Insurance" for leads.

Here's a look at the various types of insurance you may need for business and personal use.

- *Business owner's.* While there's such a thing as homebased business insurance, it's usually available only for low-traffic businesses (i.e., businesses that don't have a lot of customers coming and going in the home). In most cases, it's better to spring for traditional business owner's insurance instead, especially if you expect to have employees or independent contractors working in your home. Business owner's insurance includes coverage against physical injuries to your customers and employees, damage to their property while on your premises (such as a dent in a supplier's car when it's parked in your driveway), and other situations. This kind of coverage costs $350 to $450 per year for $500,000 of coverage from an independent agent, or $150 to $300 for $300,000 from a national company like State Farm.

Beware!

Many municipalities require push-cart vendors to have insurance for their retail operations. In Cedar Rapids, Iowa, for instance, the city requires all transient merchants to have general liability insurance in the amount of $1 million per occurrence and $1 million for property damage.

- *Commercial general liability (CGL).* CGL insurance is required for businesses that operate out of a retail space. This type of policy covers negligence, accidental damage, and personal injury (including slips and falls) at your place of business, and a policy of $1 million to $2 million is the norm, even for small businesses. If you own your building, you'll need business property (aka casualty) insurance, which protects both the building and its contents against major disasters like acts of nature (such as tornadoes), fire, vandalism, and so on. In many cases, casualty insurance is bundled in with CGL insurance. If you lease, the landlord should provide this coverage. Just be sure to get proof in writing long before you ever need it.

- *Business interruption.* This type of policy covers you in case a disability, injury, or other business interruption prevents you from working. It covers the normal cost of doing business, as well as equipment replacement, facility costs and lost income. You're more likely to need it if you own or lease a facility and/or have employees.

- *Workers' compensation.* This is a type of no-fault insurance required by all states for business owners who have employees. It pays benefits to employees who suffer work-related injuries, diseases, and illnesses. You won't need this unless you're planning to open your own factory to churn out handbags or other fashion accessories, or you plan to hire staff for a retail store.

- *Commercial auto.* If frequent travel to suppliers or manufacturing venues is on the docket in the future, you might want to upgrade your current auto insurance policy to commercial auto insurance. To save money, though, call your insurance agent and find out whether your current policy will cover you adequately while on business.

- *Disability.* This insurance replaces a certain percentage of your income if you're sidelined by an injury or illness.

- *Health.* If you don't have another wage earner in your family who can cover you while you launch your business, you'll have to get your own policy. Luckily, health insurance premiums are 100 percent deductible for self-employed business owners (and their employees, if any). Check out IRS Publication 535, *Business Expenses*, for more information.

- *Life.* Life insurance is nice to have to protect your family but not required unless you're planning to seek business financing. Then your bank probably will make it a condition for making the loan.

As you can see, it's possible to get insurance to cover practically any contingency—and of course the costs will mount up fast. Your best bet is to figure out how much risk you personally can tolerate and buy accordingly. An experienced insurance agent or broker can help you make sound decisions that take your financial status and potential for risk into account. To help you make those decisions, use the insurance worksheet below to compare prices and other options.

Insurance Planning Worksheet

Type	Required?	Monthly Premium	Annual Cost
Business owner's	Strongly recommended for homebased businesses		
Commercial general liability (CGL)	Required for brick-and-mortar stores; otherwise recommended		
Property/casualty	Required for brick-and-mortar stores		
Business interruption	No		
Workers' compensation	Yes (if you have employees)		
Commercial auto	No		
Disability	No		
Health	No		
Life	No		
Personal auto	Yes; liability in most states		
Other			
Other			
Total Annual Cost:			$

Fashion Central
Your Home Office

One of the incomparable joys of self-employment is being able to work when and where you want. Make no mistake—"self-employment" often means 18-hour days when there are orders to process or ship, or urgent paperwork to process. But who cares—when you're at the helm of your own retail empire and your commute to work is so short (saves a lot of gas!), a few extra hours a week is a price you'll probably be more than willing to pay.

Of course all this freedom also means you'll have to sacrifice a room or other space in your house for the cause. It's really important to set up an office immediately because having a dedicated space to work in will help to keep you focused even when the sun is shining and your nine iron is calling. In addition, it helps to keep you organized (translation: no lost orders, materials, or phone messages). It helps you contain your business to a single room or area so your beads, raw materials and/or inventory don't overrun your entire home. It also helps to convince people (including those pesky IRS suits) that you actually are engaged in a real profession during the day and not watching soaps or DIY Network, playing poker online, or otherwise frittering away your time.

Even if you will be opening a brick-and-mortar or click-and-brick business, you still need a home office—although not so you can work 24/7. Rather, the idea is to establish your own corporate headquarters and get your business off on the most professional footing possible.

A Place to Call Your Own

If you're sharing your living space with a loving spouse or family, it can be challenging to find a quiet area to work in. If you have a spare bedroom, you need to commandeer it now. Just swoop in, move out the TV and PlayStation, relocate the spare dresser, and donate the out-of-style clothing that's moldering in the closet. A loft or garage you can convert into usable office space is also a good option. But if you don't have a spare room, you'll have to carve out a niche in another room, most likely the den or family room. This can be problematic if your home is small or you live in an apartment, as New York jewelry retailer Ruta Fox does. Her 450-square-foot apartment is Ah Ring Central, and she admits that her business phone is 10 feet away from her bed. But basically, as long as you can designate an area that can accommodate a desk, chair, and computer, and possibly a file cabinet or bookcase, you'll be ready to roll.

One last word about family or significant others. It's really, really important to make sure every family member understands that your office area is off limits at all times, and that your business phone should *never* be answered by anyone other than yourself. Nothing will make you look more amateurish and unprofessional than

> **Bright Idea**
>
> To keep little ones occupied when you really need to concentrate on your work (or to keep them from scattering beads or other materials), assemble a "Busy Box" of quiet toys for the kids to play with only when you're trying to make calls or focus on work. Markers, coloring books, soft toys, and modeling clay are good choices.

to have your phone answered by a precocious toddler ("Can you come out and play?") or a sullen teenager (insert your own snarky comment here).

So close the door to your office at the end of the day (and put up a "Do Not Disturb" sign if necessary), or partition off your work area with a decorative screen. You could also convert a closet into a home office sanctuary by installing a desk or computer workstation, shelving and task lighting. If the closet is deep enough and has folding doors, you can leave the doors on, which will make it feel even more like a

Bright Idea

If you must have an office away from home, consider sharing space with other professionals. Brooke Sobel, the California handbag designer/manufacturer, shares a cube in an office building with several real estate professionals because she feels strongly about keeping work and home separate. Says Sobel, "I really didn't want to keep my files at home."

real office when you shut the door firmly at the end of the day. If it's not very deep, simply remove the doors and install a beautiful curtain on a tension rod as a way to "shut down" business operations at day's end. You'll find some great ideas for converting a room or a closet into a home office at HGTV.com (search on "office closet").

In this chapter, you'll find a list of the various expenses you can expect to incur when setting up a home office. Keep in mind that if you'll be opening a retail location, you'll need an office there, too, which means you'll essentially have to double your startup costs to outfit that space as well.

Tools of the Trade

Home office startup expenses fall into two categories: office equipment, including furniture and business machines like computers; and office supplies. Fortunately, you can keep expenses down right out of the box by shopping your own home for computer equipment or furniture you already own that can be commandeered. But in case you really are starting from square one, you'll find a chart on page 90 with estimates of the home office startup costs for two hypothetical businesses, as well as a worksheet on page 92 that you can use to keep track of your projected expenses as you read along. This exercise will give you a pretty good idea of whether you can swing your startup costs on your own, i.e., with paper (currency) or plastic, or whether you may need a little financing assistance.

Office Equipment

Standard office furniture is an absolute must for a home office. You'll need a desk or computer workstation, a comfortable office chair, and a sturdy two- or four-drawer file cabinet. You should also consider acquiring a bookcase so you can keep your reference materials conveniently at hand.

Office supply stores like Office Depot as well as big-box retailers like Target, Ikea, and Walmart all sell reasonably priced office furniture that will set you back as little as $50 for a basic desk (up to about $200 for a midrange desk), and $50 for a basic chair. A computer work center starts at about $90. A two-drawer letter-size file cabinet costs $40 to $100, while a four-shelf bookcase will cost around $70. To trim those costs even more, try scouring the want ads or visiting garage sales. An online auction site like eBay or the online classified site Craigslist.org are also good sources for used furniture. If your bargain buy must be shipped, make sure you factor in the cost of shipping so that a $10 steal doesn't end up costing a fortune.

Dollar Stretcher

Ikea sells wonderfully stylish modern Scandinavian office furniture on its website (ikea.com) that will really brighten up your work space without breaking the budget. Be sure to use the website's space-planning tool to figure out exactly how much furniture your new office can hold comfortably.

Personal Computer

Chances are, you already own a computer that can be pressed into service for your business. However, if you must buy one because your current computer is outdated (translation: five minutes old), you can expect to pay about $1,500 to $2,000 for a

On The Run

Since some of a designer's best ideas come while on the run, on the beach, on the phone, etc., you might prefer to invest in a laptop computer so your office will be completely portable. A loaded laptop starts at around $1,000 at a big-box retailer like Best Buy, although you can do better if you shop around. For instance, Best Buy recently offered a Toshiba U405-S2826 satellite notebook package with Vista, a built-in Web cam, and a cool fingerprint access system (for protecting confidential design files) for $849. And this was a deluxe model, with an Intel Centrino processor, 2GB DDR2 SDRAM memory, 250GB hard drive and high-speed wireless networking, built-in 5-in-1 media adapter, 13.3-inch widescreen monitor, and Intel graphics media accelerator.

Another good reason to buy a laptop is that they use much less energy than desktop computers, so you'll be doing something good for the planet while you build your business.

complete Pentium-based system that includes the hard drive, monitor, CD-RW, mouse, and printer. But there are always deals, so it pays to shop around. For instance, at the time of publication, Dell was offering the XPS 210 with a 19-inch monitor and Windows Vista at a base price of $999. (The ultimate price depends on the amount of memory and the processor you choose.)

> ### Bright Idea
> If your home office is in a carpeted room, be sure to protect your computer from being fried by purchasing an anti-static chair mat. The mat will discharge the static that will build up when a chair is moved back and forth on carpet. A can of antistatic spray will accomplish the same thing, but it has to be reapplied often.

Additional accessories and peripherals you may find handy include a flash drive (as low as $10 for 1GB of memory), a media card reader for downloading photos from your digital camera to your computer (about $20 for an external model), a scanner (as low as $100), a mouse pad ($3 and up), and a surge protector for each of your peripherals ($15 to $50).

Software

You'll need standard productivity software to run your business empire, including Microsoft Office and Intuit QuickBooks. Office Professional 2007 includes Word, Excel, PowerPoint, Access, Accounting Express, Outlook and Publisher and retails for $500. (The Mac version is Office Mac, which includes Word, Excel, PowerPoint, and Entourage, and retails for around $350.) QuickBooks is an easy-to-use accounting package that helps you organize your business finances and perform day-to-day tasks like printing invoices and checks, managing your business checking account and more. QuickBooks Pro retails for around $200. If a retail store is in your immediate future, Intuit recommends QuickBooks Premier, which offers more advanced features like inventory cost tracking and sales expense forecasts; the Premier edition is $500.

If your plans include designing fashion accessories, then you also should invest in Adobe Photoshop CS4. This is the product that Colorado scarf designer David Kulaas uses to transform his wildflower photos into the digital art that graces his stunning silk scarves. If you don't have graphic design experience, you may need to take a course to learn how to use this design powerhouse, but Kulaas assures us that it's fairly user-friendly. The software retails for $699.

Phones and Answering Machines

If you're planning to use a landline as your business phone (recommended), you should invest in the most expensive business phone you can afford, which will give you the best sound and transmission quality possible. A standard two-line speakerphone

Beware!

VoIP technology is certainly very cool and definitely cheaper than traditional phone service, but some providers limit you to calling only subscribers to the same service. So when you check into VoIP service, be sure to ask whether you can call any phone number. If not, then try another provider with fewer restrictions.

(one line for the business and one for personal) with auto-redial, memory dial, flashing lights, mute button, and other useful features will cost $40 to $150. The office superstores offer a wide range of high-quality phones, as does Hello Direct (800-Hello-34, hellodirect.com), which specializes in business telecom equipment at many price points. (One line to check out is the Polycom line of professional business phones.) And while you're at it, consider purchasing a phone with a headset for hands-free calling so you can prevent the discomfort caused by cradling the receiver between your neck and shoulder.

Of course, the latest in communication is Voice-over-Internet-Protocol (VoIP), which allows you to make phone calls using a broadband internet connection rather than a standard analog phone line. But you'll need a VoIP-enabled phone to access the service. Hello Direct offers the Packet8 Virtual Office VoIP Business Phone System, which comes with features like free activation, unlimited calling, business-class voice mail, and three phones. It retails for $379.

While voice mail is the choice of most people these days for taking messages, you may find that that old workhorse, the answering machine, is still your message buddy of choice. Its chief advantage over voice mail is that you can screen incoming calls audibly, which comes in handy when a caller blocks his number on your Caller ID device. At $15 to $65 for a basic model, answering machines may be the last great technology bargain, although you can pay up to $200 for a model with advanced features and a built-in phone.

Cellular Phone

At the rate the phone company is adding new area codes, it seems pretty obvious that most people have a cell phone. But if you don't, you definitely should get one so you don't miss any calls from prospects when you're on the road visiting clients, or so you can keep in touch with your manufacturing facility or vendors no matter where you happen to be. Most cellular service providers offer a free basic phone at the time of service activation, which is a bit lower on the coolness scale but functional nonetheless. If you've always wanted an iPhone to manage day-to-day details, surf the internet, and retrieve e-mail, then you're in luck—the price has now dropped to about $199, down from $599 for the 8GB model. As with any cellular phone, you'll pay a service activation fee of about $40, plus standard monthly access fees.

Another viable communication option is the BlackBerry (blackberry.com), a combination e-mail, Bluetooth-enabled cell phone, wireless internet, IM, and paging device that's a slightly clunkier cousin of the iPhone. The basic model is cheaper than an iPhone at around $150, but you can quickly ratchet up the price by adding extra features. It also has a service activation fee and monthly access fees of $40 or more.

> ### Bright Idea
>
> If you don't own one already, invest in a digital camera so you can take pictures of the accessories you create as you finish them, both for posting on your website and as a visual archive. If you'll be photographing small items like earrings, purchase a tabletop tripod so your pictures will be sharp and crisp.

Copy Machine

If there's a quickie print shop like FedEx Office's or Speedy Printing near your home office, then you don't necessarily need your own copy machine. But if you're designing fashion accessories or will be printing line sheets on demand, you might find it very convenient to have one. They're really reasonable, too—as little as $100 to $500 for a standard desktop machine, or up to $2,000 for a stand-alone model that reduces, enlarges, sorts, collates, and makes double-sided copies. In addition to electricity they need toner cartridges, which sell for about $10 to $15 at office supply stores and online.

One really cool model to check out, if you have the startup funds, is the Xerox 4150, which retails for $2,400 and up and includes a duplex copier with a finisher that collates and staples, a scanner with scan-to-e-mail, a fax with fax-to-e-mail capability, password protection, and more.

Postal Scales and Meters

Most homebased fashion accessories entrepreneurs tend to be jacks-and-jills-of-all-trades, which includes taking orders and shipping out the merchandise. If that sounds like your lot in life, too, you definitely need to invest in a postal scale to make sure you're affixing enough postage to your outgoing mail. You simply weigh the package, then go to the U.S. Postal Service's site at usps.com, buy online postage, then use your computer to print out mailing labels. A mechanical scale ($10 to $25) works fine if you'll be mailing only a few items per day. If you'll be mailing in larger quantities regularly (and one can hope that will happen sooner rather than later), you'll be better served by a digital scale, which runs $40 to $200. Finally, if you think you'll be using priority or expedited mailing services regularly, a programmable electronic scale is usually your best bet and runs $70 to $250.

An alternative to buying postage from the dear old USPS is the Pitney Bowes Stamp Expressions postage printer, a $160 stand-alone scale with a small footprint that's great for mailing letters and small packages in small quantities. As with the USPS, you purchase online postage right from your desktop. See pitneybowes.com for more info.

If you think you'll be mailing larger packages (full of purses, for example) and lots of them, you might want to invest in an all-in-one digital postage meter like the Mailstation2 digital mailing system from Pitney Bowes. You rent the Mailstation2 (since you can't own a postage meter because of USPS regulations) for about $19.95 a month, plus the cost of postage, which is available for purchase online 24/7.

Point-of-Sale Equipment

Whether you're shipping accessories from the comfort of your home office, selling from a brick-and-mortar location, or raking in online orders, it's pretty much a given that you'll have to accept credit and debit cards. The equipment that allows you to do that is a point-of-sale (POS) terminal. This little box is used to verify electronically whether a customer's credit is good before concluding a transaction, and it requires a credit card receipt printer. They cost around $299 and $195, respectively.

Alternatively, there are POS terminals that have the printer built in, like the Hypercom T7P Standard ($229 and up), as well as wireless POS terminals, which require cellular service to work and start at around $995. Finally, the most cost-effective way to process credit cards and print receipts is by using a PC-based software program that you install on your home (or store) computer. A few POS software packages to check out include PcCharge (Verifone, pccharge.com, around $250) and ICVerify (ICVerify, icverify.com, $250 for a single-user license, starting at $375 for the multiuser product).

One more thing you'll need to clear both credit and debit card purchases is a merchant account. After paying about $100 to establish a new merchant account, you'll incur per-transaction fees. You'll find more information about merchant accounts in Chapter 16.

Office Supplies

If you already have a stash of pads, pens, file folders, Post-Its, CD-RWs, and other office supplies lying around the house, round them up now so you can save a few bucks on office supplies. But if you don't have enough stuff to fill up the drawers in your desk, you'll probably need about $150 to stock up on the necessities, which should hold you for a while. While you're at the office superstore, order your business cards and stationery. To give your budding fashion accessories business the upscale look it needs and deserves, buy the finest stationery and business cards you can afford, which in the scheme of things really doesn't amount to a huge outlay of cash. You can expect to fork out about $80 for 250 one-color premium stationery sheets, $85 for 250 envelopes and

$35 for 250 business cards. Alternatively, you can check out the multitude of online printing companies that have a wide selection of paper and printing styles and colors from which to choose. You'll find a list of printers in the Appendix.

White, cream, and gray stock will give your stationery and cards an elegant look. If you're going for funky or edgy, try color and graphics. But don't go too wild with typefaces. After all, you want your customers to be able to decipher your contact information.

Commercial Mailbox

Since it's highly unlikely that you'll ever see fashion accessories customers in your home office, you may wish to give serious consideration to renting a commercial mailbox for your business mail. In addition to keeping your business mail separate from your personal correspondence and bills, a commercial mailbox allows you to keep your home address private (a really good idea in these days of rampant identify theft).

Ye Olde Reliable-If-Expensive USPS will happily rent you a 3-by-5.5-inch P.O. box for $9 to $37 for six months, while a box at a commercial mail center like Mailboxes Etc. runs $10 to $20 a month depending on the size of the box. While there's no stigma attached to using a P.O. box for business mail, if you use a mail center box, your customer will never know because mail is addressed to an actual street address rather than a P.O. box number. If you'd like more specifics, check out usps.com or mailboxesetc.com.

Just the Fax, Ma'am

Some people think fax machines are old technology, but let's face it—if you want to send a prospective buyer a line sheet, it's usually better to fax it because so many people refuse to open computer attachments due to the risk of computer viruses. In addition, you'll find that a lot of mom-and-pop businesses just aren't all that tech-savvy, so their owners actually may prefer to receive a fax.

Fax machines are really inexpensive and do much more than just fax documents—they also serve as scanners, copiers, and printers. You can find a standard fax machine for as little as $100 or one of the multifunction machines for $200 and up. It's recommended that you install your fax on a dedicated phone line if you intend to keep it on all the time to capture those all-important incoming orders. You can expect to pay $40 to $60 for phone line installation, plus the cost of monthly service (usually around $40 per line).

▲

The Moment of Truth

You probably can tell simply by reading through this chapter that it won't take much cash to set up a home office for your fashion accessories business, especially if you already have the big-ticket items like a computer and its accompanying peripherals. Even if you do need a computer, you may find you can fund the entire setup with plastic or savings. But if you're really starting on a shoestring, or your other startup costs (like for manufacturing) will be high, you may find you need a little financial boost. You'll find a discussion of financing options in Chapter 16 of this book.

Office Equipment and Supplies Sample Costs

	Low	High
Office Equipment		
Computer, printer		$1,500
Software		
Microsoft Office		$500
QuickBooks Pro	$200	
QuickBooks Premier		$500
POS software	$250	
Photoshop CS3		$649
General Office		
Surge protector		$15
UPS (for battery backup)	$60	$200
Multipurpose fax/scanner/copier	$200	$200
Copy machine	$100	$500
Phone	$40	$150
Postal scale	$40	$160
Digital camera	$130	$350

Office Equipment and Supplies Sample Costs, continued

	Low	High
General Office		
Answering machine*	$25	
POS terminal		$299
Calculator	$10	$10
Office Furniture		
Desk	$50	$250
Chair	$50	$100
File cabinet(s)	$40	$100
Bookcase(s)	$70	$70
Chair mat		$16
Office Supplies		
Business cards, stationery	$200	$200
Line sheets	$100	$100
Miscellaneous supplies (pens, folders, etc.)	$50	$50
Computer/copier paper	$25	$25
Extra printer cartridges	$80	$80
Extra fax cartridges	$90	$90
Extra copier toner	$10	$10
CD-RW disks	$25	$25
Mouse pad		$3
TOTAL	**$1,845**	**$6,152**

Note: It's assumed that the low-end business will already have a suitable computer system that can be used for the business, which helps keep startup costs low.

*The high-end business has voice mail so it doesn't need an answering machine.

Office Equipment and Supplies Worksheet

Office Equipment	
Computer, printer	$
Software	
Microsoft Office	$
QuickBooks Pro	$
QuickBooks Premier	$
POS software	$
Photoshop CS3	$
General Office	
Surge protector	$
UPS (for battery backup)	$
Multipurpose fax/scanner/copier	$
Copy machine	$
Phone	$
Postal scale	$
Digital camera	$
Answering machine	$
POS terminal	$
Calculator	$
Office Furniture	
Desk	$
Chair	$
File cabinet(s)	$
Bookcase(s)	$
Chair mat	$
Office Supplies	
Business cards, stationery	$
Line sheets	$
Miscellaneous supplies (pens, folders, etc.)	$
Computer/copier paper	$
Extra printer cartridges	$
Extra fax cartridges	$
Extra copier toner	$
CD-RW disks	$
Mouse pad	$
TOTAL	**$**

Going
to the Source

Once you have a place to work and a good idea of what your market looks like, your next step should be to find products to sell. Basically, you have three options: You can design and make your own one-of-a-kind custom accessories with components available domestically or abroad; you can design (or have someone else design) fashion accessories that will be produced under your direction by a contract manufacturer; or you can purchase ready-made fashion accessories at wholesale prices and resell them at retail prices, usually through an online or brick-and-mortar store. You also can do a combination of these methods, as does one of the entrepreneurs we interviewed. First and foremost she is a designer who designs fashion accessories that are manufactured for her and sold on her website and in her store, but she also purchases other pieces that complement her custom work direct from manufacturers, then resells them. Because the accessories are deliberately chosen so they relate to each other, the finished product line has the look of a collection.

In this chapter, you'll find information about how to find supplies for making custom accessories, how to locate ready-made accessories, and how to manufacture accessories to your specifications.

Accessory Supply Sources

Finding sources for the components you'll need to make jewelry and other fashion accessories isn't a problem—but deciding among them could be because there are so many. To make the job more manageable, start with The National Craft Association's wholesale directory listings at craftassoc.org. The association offers affordable directories for jewelry-making supplies and materials ($14.95 for nonmembers), arts and crafts supplies ($49.95) and general craft supplies ($26.95). It also has a nationwide directory of craft malls and consignment shops ($24.95), an artisans' guide to shops and galleries ($26.95), and a nationwide directory of mail order catalogs ($19.95) that you can use to market your products.

To take a free exploratory tour of the supply market, see if your local library has a copy of *The Catalog of Catalogs VI: The Complete Mail Order Directory* by Edward Palder, which lists 15,000 different catalogs in more than 900 subject areas in its 567 pages; or the *Crafts Supply Source Book* by Margaret Boyd, which is a mail order guide to craft materials. Both of these books were last published in 1999 so some of the contact information is probably pretty outdated, but they're still useful for finding the names of companies that sell what you need, which you then can research on the internet.

Beware!
The auction site eBay is a good source of wholesale goods—beads, in particular. Just be sure to factor in the cost of shipping before you commit to buying. A shipping cost that's very high (which often reflects a combination of shipping costs plus eBay's various fees) can wipe out your profitability.

Of course, the internet is an awesome resource all by itself. Some wholesale resources we uncovered after doing just a casual Google search include:

- *Go Wholesale.* For miscellaneous craft supplies (gowholesale.com)
- *My Bead Point.* Based in Singapore; offers higher-end beading materials like Swarovski crystals, semiprecious gems, and cloisonné beads (mybeadpoint.com)
- *Siegel of California.* Wholesale leather and supply source (siegelofca.com)
- *Tandy Leather Factory.* Source of wholesale leather (tandyleatherfactory.com)
- *Wholesalers Catalog.* A list of wholesalers and manufacturers (wholesalers catalog.com)

Of course, while you can find just about anything you need on the internet, you also should try to do your buying as close to home as possible, both to save on shipping costs and to support the local economy. If you live in or near a fashion epicenter like Los Angeles or New York, you'll have plenty of wholesale resources from which to select. But many other large metropolitan areas also have wholesale supply companies, so check your local Yellow Pages or go to Whitepages.com to search for "wholesale craft supplies" or "wholesale jewelry supplies."

If you buy in sufficient quantities, you should be able to negotiate good discounts on whatever you need. But research prices on the internet before you buy locally so if there's room to negotiate, you'll know how much things cost and you can make a reasonable offer that's more likely to be accepted.

Bright Idea

The best way to find a reputable overseas manufacturer is through referrals. Talk to other small-business owners who manufacture products; chat up your materials supplier; or call domestic manufacturers at random and ask about their overseas sources. Generally speaking, people are happy to help, and you can feel confident about the vetted sources those conversations yield.

Ready-Made

If you're planning to buy wholesale fashion accessories products that can be sold in your retail or virtual store, you'll find there's a breathtaking array of sources for whatever you need. As before, start with domestic resources whenever possible. You can find them easily in the Yellow Pages or online. But if you can't find what you want locally, you definitely should look at international sources. China, in particular, is a major supplier of fashion accessories, although other parts of Southeast Asia, including Bali and Thailand, are big suppliers of sterling silver jewelry and other accessories.

To start your search, try Global Sources (globalsources.com), which provides a comprehensive and constantly updated list of verified suppliers. (This is where David Kulaas, the Colorado scarf designer, started his search for a manufacturing facility.) And the list

▲

is massive. Since you could spend a lot of time trying to sift through all the new stuff, you'll want to subscribe to Global Sources' products e-mail list so you can be notified when new products are added. The site also provides information about upcoming fashion accessories fairs you might like to visit to search for the next must-have fashion accessory.

Another source that deserves a look is the Hong Kong Trade Development Council (hktdc.com). In addition to links to suppliers, you'll find a wealth of useful information, including e-commerce business tools, market intelligence, and a list of worldwide trade events. This site has a huge number of suppliers, too—for example, there were 134 pages of handbags alone from which to choose.

A third promising source to explore is Alibaba.com (alibaba.com). This site claims to be the world's largest business-to-business marketplace for importers and exporters, with more than 200 countries and territories represented—including the United States, by the way, so be sure to consider red, white, and blue, too. By becoming a member (at no charge), you'll have full access to the site, which includes being able to post specialty purchase requests.

Finally, although you can easily do all your buying halfway around the world from your home office, it's usually a good idea to visit one or two international trade fairs to get an idea of what's available before you make final inventory decisions. Naturally, this is not an inexpensive proposition—you'll rack up the types of expenses typical for any business trip, including airfare, accommodations, and meals. But there's no substitute for seeing things in person. So if at all possible, build some funds into your startup budget so you can make the trek to the Far East.

Make Your Own

While it's possible to handcraft or hand-tool exquisite fashion accessories and be justifiably proud of every item you produce, let's face it: You're only one person and you can only create so many items in your own little workshop, even with the assistance of part-time sewing employees. So you may have to make the monumental decision to manufacture your own products.

This is not a decision to be made lightly. Manufacturing is complicated, time-consuming and expensive. But for an entrepreneur with big ideas, it may be the only way to turn dreams into reality.

One huge piece of advice that you'll want to highlight, underscore, and otherwise mark in permanent ink: If you intend to go the manufacturing route, use a contract manufacturer, which is a company that makes products that are marketed and sold by another company (you, in this case). In essence, you're contracting for the use of the manufacturer's equipment for a set period of time (i.e., long enough to make your product). If you try to set up your own manufacturing facility, you'll encounter towering startup costs and manufacturing problems that you don't need as a fledgling fashion entrepreneur.

Smart Tip

U.S. agents or brokers who represent foreign manufacturers are great sources of manufacturing leads. They'll also have the inside track on issues like importing and quotas. A good place to meet these reps is at fashion accessories trade shows, so be sure to plan a trip to a show early in your startup phase.

Finding a manufacturer—even one overseas—is actually not all that daunting. All the sources mentioned earlier relating to product acquisition can steer you to a contract manufacturer, or you can Google to find others. In addition, don't forget to scour both the New York and Los Angeles garment districts for leads. For instance, by Googling "handbag patternmaker" we immediately found a luxury New York City handbag and belt manufacturer online that specializes in small-to-midsize domestic handbag and leather product development, pattern making, sample making, manufacturing, contracting, consulting, and sourcing.

While it's better for America to buy American, you're likely to find that oversees manufacturing is less expensive. Brooke Sobel, the San Francisco handbag designer, says that in her experience, not only is China less expensive—for example, labor is $15 an hour vs. $40 an hour stateside—the quality is also better than what she found in Los Angeles. "It depends who you use," she says, "but I found that even though you have to wait for samples and product to arrive from China, it's never late and the quality often is better."

But of course there are challenges inherent in working with an overseas company, including long lead times, time zone differences, language barriers, and lengthy wait for deliveries. Donna von Hoesslin, the California belt and jewelry designer, once had to go back to the drawing board, literally, when the production manager she so carefully recruited in Southeast Asia saw how much work was involved in the production of her accessories and backed out. "I had to find someone quickly to rescue my business," she says.

Nevertheless, you really don't have to be afraid of working with a foreign manufacturer. These days, companies abroad are very adept at making the production process work from afar, and as long as you have enough time built into your schedule to have products shipped to you before seasonal launches, everything should work out fine.

Whether you ultimately decide to stick with a domestic manufacturer or seek one abroad, it's usually a good idea to locate a couple of potential manufacturers in this fact-finding phase. Compare their capabilities, their skill and reputation, and their turnaround time. Above all, decide which one seems easiest to work with and most willing to please you. That goes a long way toward establishing a satisfactory business relationship.

Before you discuss your products and ideas in detail, it's important to have a representative from the factories that will be bidding on your business sign a nondisclosure agreement (NDA). This is important because there are copycats out there just waiting to swoop in and steal your best ideas. An NDA isn't ironclad, especially if you're dealing with someone in a foreign country, but it does send a signal to the factory that you're a serious businessperson. Your attorney can draw up a simple NDA for you.

From Idea to Product

Once you've weighed quotes, reviewed manufacturing schedules, and selected a manufacturer, you'll follow these 10 basic steps to produce your fashion accessories:

1. *Design the product(s), or have them designed for you.* Be sure to do this electronically, using a CAD (computer aided design) program, Illustrator, or other design software program so the designs can be transmitted back and forth electronically. If you'll be producing a sewn product like a handbag or belt, you'll need a pattern maker, as well. The pattern maker uses your design specs (or the specs that have been created to your specifications) to whip up a pattern that can be sewn perfectly. As part of the process, the pattern maker will report back to you on any obvious problems that may exist in the design so time isn't wasted making prototypes (or worse yet, an entire production line) that won't turn out correctly. As you can imagine, a good pattern maker is worth his/her weight in gold. Be prepared to pay $40 or more an hour for a pattern maker's services, and don't forget to ask how much experience the person has, as well as for references.

2. *Research materials needed for production.* This includes material like leather or vinyl, as well as hardware for handbags (zippers, buckles, etc.); beads, gemstones, wire, clasps, and other findings for jewelry; leather and other materials for belts; yarn or silk for scarves, etc. Don't forget that your factory will only be making the products—it will be up to you to order and ship the raw production materials there. That's why it's usually a good idea to find a materials source near your factory, if at all possible. It will save both time and money.

3. *Get samples.* Order fabric and sample materials from the suppliers you choose.

4. *Have prototypes (aka sample sets) made from sample materials.* There are a number of "cut-and-sew" companies in the United States that work with small and startup companies and can create prototypes to your specifications. (Google "contract sewing" for leads.) Usually you have to provide an initial prototype from the pattern for the cut-and-sew company to work with. Once they're finalized, these prototypes ultimately will be sent to the manufacturer as reference before and during production.

> **Tip...**
>
> **Smart Tip**
>
> If you have the talent, skills, and time, you can make your prototypes yourself. For example, a jewelry designer can easily mock up necklace or earring prototypes, while a handbag or bag designer with sewing skills can whip up bags. You'll usually need about a dozen prototypes; some for practice and some to send to the factory as reference.

5. *Order production materials so you'll be ready to go when the production pattern is finalized.* Create a timeline with lead times on delivery of raw materials to the factory. This is especially important if you're working with a supplier that's out of the country.

6. *Wait anxiously while the prototypes are being made.* This is a good time to think about marketing strategies for rolling out your products, create line sheets, review your financing options, and/or obtain signed NDAs.

7. *Inspect prototypes you've received and put them through rigorous quality control procedures.* If you're producing sewn products like scarves, inspect the rolled hems for evidence of fraying. If you're making handbags, you need to zip and unzip, latch and unlatch, and otherwise test every part of the bag for stress points, faulty construction and so on. If you're making jewelry, you must be sure that spring ring clasps are sturdy, beads are uniform in color and size, etc.

   This phase is also your chance to make any design tweaks. For example, if you decide that the drop on a handbag strap is too long, you can still direct the factory to make a change. You can also reject any products that don't live up to your expectations, although it will cost you to go back to the drawing board. Just remember: If the quality isn't up to snuff, you must speak up now or forever hold your peace.

8. *Approve the prototype(s).* Then give the factory the go-ahead to produce final samples.

9. *Wait some more until the production samples arrive.*

10. *Approve the samples.* Let production begin!

Be sure you work enough time into your delivery schedule to accommodate all these production steps. For example, here's Reagan Hardy and Emmie Howard's typical manufacturing production schedule: The Georgia manufacturers of men's belts, hats, and other accessories wait three to four weeks to get fabric samples (called a strike-off) from their silk printers in Asia. Once the samples have been approved, it takes another three to four weeks for the screen printing to be completed, then another three to four weeks to get the product manufactured. And this doesn't even include design time, which of course also has to be worked into the schedule.

While it's best to leave production matters to the factory—under your direction, of course—you do have to keep an eye on things, as Ruta Fox, the New York jewelry entrepreneur, discovered. She worked with the same manufacturer for years, but one year learned that it was moving its operations to Florida by the end of November.

Foreign Shores

Here's a list of helpful websites and publications for doing business abroad:

- ○ *China Sourcing Fairs.* A list of product trade shows, including fashion accessories; visit tradeshow.globalsources.com.
- ○ *Export.gov.* Information about how customs brokers and freight forwarders can help you land products manufactured overseas.
- ○ *ExportBureau.com.* An online dictionary of trade, shipping, and export terms.
- ○ *Travel.State.gov.* The U.S. Department of State's online source for travel advisories and warnings so you don't boldly go where Uncle Sam doesn't want you to go.
- ○ *U.S. Customs and Border Protection.* Contains plenty of background information and tips; visit cbp.gov and click on the "Trade" tab on the toolbar, then "Basic Importing and Exporting."
- ○ *U.S. Department of State.* Offers tips for Americans traveling abroad, including how to apply for a passport; see travel.state.gov.
- ○ *U.S. Department of State Background Notes.* Everything you ever wanted to know about dozens of countries around the world; includes information on the land, people, history, economy, political conditions, and travel and business information, as well as a delightful look at each country's nuclear and chemical weapons arsenals; located at state.gov.
- ○ *U.S. Office of Commercial and Business Affairs.* Offers advice on doing business in international markets; see state.gov.

She needed her inventory by November 1st so she figured all would be well—until she discovered that the manufacturer's whole building had been packed up and everything was on a truck headed for the Sunshine State. Worse yet, they couldn't find her merchandise. So Fox went to The Jewelers' Vigilance Committee (JVC), which mediates for jewelers, to file a grievance. "I had a lot of orders but I didn't have an endless amount of capital to replace those rings," Fox says. "I had to buy new sets of diamonds to make up new rings, which almost put me out of business. Luckily, the JVC mediated for me to get hold of the company owner and get my money back, so I didn't have to hire an attorney."

You can find out more about the JVC at jvclegal.org.

Adventures in Customs Land

If you're manufacturing goods overseas, there's one last thing you have to be concerned about: getting them to the United States so you can sell them online or in your store. You can expect to incur duties and customs fees, as well as extra costs like insurance and delivery charges. Sometimes the factory will build the cost of these extras into its quote, but you need to know that upfront so you don't get a nasty surprise when the products show up at a Chinese port instead of on the friendly shores of the United States as you expected.

Customs issues are too complex for us to tackle in a book of this size. But basically this is what happens: Let's say you're manufacturing handbags in China that will enter the United States at the Port of Los Angeles, then will be transported overland to your store in Kansas City. If your manufacturer quotes terms like FOB China, that means it will pay the delivery "freight on board" charges as far as the Chinese port of embarkation. If the terms are FOB Los Angeles, that means the transportation charges are paid as far as the Los Angeles port.

If your terms are FOB China, you'll need a customs broker to estimate the landed costs of the goods, then enter and clear the merchandise through customs for you. Then you'll need a freight forwarder to ship the merchandise to you. To make the process easier, look for a company that handles both tasks (Google either or both terms for leads).

For the whole scoop on importing products, check out Entrepreneur's *Start Your Own Import/Export Business*.

UPC Codes

As a consumer you're probably very familiar with Universal Product Codes (UPCs), the 12-digit codes that appear on virtually every product sold in stores. The code, which is usually accompanied by a bar code, consists of numbers and dashes that

Smart Tip

Tip...

If you'll be selling primarily to small-business owners, like boutiques and gift shops, or at street fairs or craft shows, it's not necessary to have UPCs for your fashion accessories. However, you'll have to devise some method for keeping track of your products and inventory levels. You might just find that UPCs are the best way to do that after all.

identify both a company and its products. If you'll be selling to large retailers, it will be absolutely necessary for you to have UPCs for every product, since stores rely on bar codes for everything from keeping reliable inventory counts to managing logistics.

Fortunately, it's easy to get these digital designators. To apply, visit GS1, the Supreme Global Keeper of the Order of UPC, at gs1us.org, then click on "BarCodes and eCom" on the menu on the right-hand side. You'll have to fill out an application to obtain a unique GS1 company prefix and a UPC company prefix that will be used to create UPCs. The fee for this service ranges from $150 to $1,500 per GS1 company prefix, depending on your company's gross sales revenues—or projected revenues, for a new company. (Luckily, it's a one-time deal.) Your application will be processed in about two business days, after which you'll receive materials from GS1 about how to create unique codes. Finally, you'll need a vendor who can print the high-quality bar codes that will be affixed to your products. GS1 helpfully provides an online certified products and services directory that will give you leads to a vendor.

For more information about UPCs, go to the GS1 website and review its various educational materials.

Sale
Away

Nailing down the details about where you'll obtain or manufacture your merchandise is a huge step forward in bringing your fashion accessories to market. The next logical step in the development of your business is to figure out exactly where you'll sell those products.

A lot of entrepreneurs who are new to the sales arena start out by marketing their goods in small venues like craft shows and street festivals. This is a good idea for a number of reasons. First, these types of sales channels bring you face-to-face with your customers—people who will probably have lots to say about what you have for sale. For example, they might ask whether your [fill in the blank here] comes in more than one color or a larger (or smaller) size, or whether there are coordinating pieces, and so on. This is invaluable feedback that can help you determine which way to take your product line in the future. For instance, if you discover you haven't sold a single pair of the sparkly shark tooth earrings you thought were so cool, but the local Goth teens are snapping up your braided leather belts to use as chokers, then you can adjust your inventory the next time you go to a craft show in their neighborhood.

Second, a smaller venue is a good place to get your feet wet. There's a knack to selling that you'll develop as you go along. Interacting with small groups or single customers will help you learn how to pitch your accessories without being pushy or obnoxious, and without the pressure of juggling many customers at once.

A smaller venue like a craft show isn't as intimidating to a new business owner. Craft shows and street fairs tend to be friendlier and more relaxed than, say, an accessories trade show like MAGIC. (Not that they're always small—Liza Sonia Wallach, the California jewelry designer, has had good success exhibiting at the Union Street Fair in San Francisco, which has 150 craft booths.)

Starting small also is good for your peace of mind. Because let's be honest: While you may be very hopeful that your accessories will become the latest rage and you'll make a fortune, at the same time you can't help but worry that at the end of the day you won't have made a discernible dent in your inventory. Then your next concern will be, "How will I make my next mortgage payment?" This is exactly why it was recommended in Chapter 1 that you consider starting your business on a part-time basis. It's always helpful when you start a new business to have another job that pays the bills, unless you have a considerable nest egg stashed away somewhere or a spouse who is willing to take care of the finances until your business gains ground.

Ways to Make a Sale

There actually is an astonishing number of sales channels available to fashion accessories entrepreneurs. While it's possible to sell in

> **Tip...**
>
> **Smart Tip**
>
> A resource you might find helpful if you're interested in selling accessories to small shops and boutiques is the *Artisans Nationwide Guide to Shops and Galleries*. It's available from the National Craft Association for $26.95 for non-members at its website at craftassoc.org.

Smart Tip

The National Craft Association publishes a nationwide directory of craft malls and consignment shops you might find helpful when deciding where to sell your fashion accessories. The directory is available to nonmembers for $24.95 at the association's website at craftassoc.org.

more than one at a time, new business owners generally start out with a single sales outlet, then expand to encompass others as their sales—and confidence—grow. These sales venues include:

Craft Shows and Craft Malls

Some business owners turn their noses up at what are perceived to be homespun little venues, but the reality is, they're not as low caliber as you might think, plus they're the perfect place to learn the business of selling while actually making money. But here's a really important secret to success: You need to pick the right show. Sounds obvious, but *not* picking the right show is a common mistake among new business owners who are desperate to make sales. That means no high school fundraisers or show with just a handful of booths (unless they're on Rodeo Drive or Fifth Avenue, that is). It also means, for example, that if you're selling high-end gold jewelry with inlaid semi-precious gems, you skip the shows that feature crocheted doilies and inexpensive costume jewelry from China.

So do your homework and find out what types of businesses will be exhibiting and what they sell. A good choice is a show that features handcrafted items like yours, although you'll want to find out how many other jewelry (or handbag, belt, or scarf) designers/sellers will also be exhibiting. It's good to have competition, but if the competition is too fierce, you run the risk of not standing out in the crowd.

Craft malls are similar to craft shows insofar as they offer booth space to artisans like you. However, craft malls usually rent space to exhibitors on a longer-term basis—say, by the month or year. Oftentimes the mall is open limited hours, so you have time to spend doing other things. Some malls will even handle sales transactions for you when you're not actually onsite (because they know you don't want to spend your every waking hour in your booth). This gives your accessories needed exposure and increases the possibility of sales.

Street Festivals and Art Fairs

These types of sales venues are hot-hot-hot across the country, and not just because they tend to take place during the summer months. It's not unusual for them to attract thousands

Smart Tip

For a list of street fairs, go to Local.com, then type in the term "street fair" and the city and state you're interested in. The list is remarkably complete and comes with clickable links to contact information, a map, and reviews by past attendees.

of visitors over a two- or three-day period. They also usually feature an eclectic mix of merchandise, from food to candles to Harley-Davidson vests. As with a craft show, you should do some due diligence to find out what kinds of small businesses have exhibited in the past to see if the fair is a good fit for your high-end merchandise. Also, if you're a jewelry designer making one-of-a-kind items, or if you offer hand-painted items like scarves or hand-beaded items such as belts, you might find that an art fair is a great place to show your products because your status as an artisan will appeal to the art lovers in attendance.

Vendor Carts

If you've ever cruised an urban landscape like Manhattan, then you're familiar with vendor carts (aka push carts). But we're not talking about hot dog stands here—rather, we're referring to stand-alone carts that are used to display merchandise, usually in malls. If you'd like to try this method of advertising your products, go to the most upscale mall in your community—preferably one that has very high-end department stores—and inquire about the availability of vendor carts. But don't even think about buying your own. Contracting with a mall management company that leases or rents the carts to small-business owners is the way to go. The idea here is to test the market and get a bunch of revenue streams going for your new business, not make a career out of selling off a cart.

Wholesale

Selling products wholesale may be the best way to break into the fashion accessories market. By wholesale we mean selling merchandise in large quantities to a retailer, who in turn sells the merchandise to the end consumer. This actually is an enviable position to be in because you don't have to deal with onesie-twosie sales to end consumers like you do with a brick-and-mortar or virtual retail store (both viable and both discussed later, by the way). Rather, you sell several or many products to a single retailer, who in turn has to do the advertising and marketing to move the product on his/her end. You're out of the picture until the request comes in for a new shipment of whatever it is that you sell.

Experienced fashion-accessories entrepreneurs heartily recommend the wholesale style of business. "Wholesale is cleaner than retail, especially for a small operation," says David Kulaas, the Colorado silk scarf designer. "Overall it's easier than dealing with individual buyers."

But approach is everything, according to Liza Sonia Wallach, the California jewelry designer. "Never say you're a new designer when you walk into a store," she warns. "Just say, 'I'm a local designer, and I'd like to make an appointment to show you my line.' If they know you're new they may want to take items on consignment instead of buying them outright. Also, I found that Monday is the very best day to make cold calls."

Cold calls are just the beginning. Once you've piqued the interest of a retailer, you have to deliver on your promises to have merchandise in his or her hands on a set schedule. You have to follow up with active prospects who are interested but not yet ready to buy. You also have to keep meticulous records on who has which merchandise, who has paid, and who's in arrears.

The result of all that effort can be phenomenal, as Reagan Hardy and Emmie Howard of Southern Proper discovered. The Georgia-based partners now have their products in nearly 150 stores across the country, all of which was made possible through sweat equity—i.e., stumping for stores and making cold calls. They also undertake grassroots marketing campaigns, like their fall "Tailgates and Ties" tour, which targets their retailers in college towns, and their spring "Steeplechase" tour, during which they attend various horse races around the Southeast to promote the Southern Proper brand and meet their customers.

"You have to harass buyers but in a nice way," adds Brooke Sobel, the California handbag designer. "And you have to be persistent. Buyers are busy people, but they like hearing from designers. Just be aware that nothing happens overnight. You have to keep knocking on doors, showing your line sheet and samples, and making calls."

Department Stores

Department stores just might be the Holy Grail of Retail-dom. If you can convince a buyer to stock your accessories, you get instant visibility, and you're often featured in multiple stores. You'll benefit from the store's advertising efforts, which drive people in to see what you offer. You'll also get to-die-for sales volume. However, you'll find that department stores are some of the more difficult places to infiltrate. For one thing, buyers are interested in products that sell immediately, and since new product lines take time to catch on, they might be leery about taking a chance on your untested accessories. Also, department stores usually need large quantities of merchandise, which can be problematic for a small artisan or manufacturer. And it's not just producing the quantity that's the problem—it's financing the production of the item so you can sell it to a department store.

Then there are chargebacks, the bane of a wholesaler's existence. Chargebacks are nasty little penalties assessed by retailers (usually the big players but sometimes even the smaller chains) that are not happy with some aspect of the wholesale transaction. For example, if the retailer feels that you didn't label the box or the contents correctly—zap. You're assessed a chargeback. Or maybe you used a different font on the package labels than the one your contract specified—bam. That could cost you $150. And heaven forbid if you're late: That could be another $150. Because of this, Wallach stresses that it's imperative to carefully read the list of specifications provided to you and follow them to the letter. Otherwise, if you accidentally do something as innocent as use 7-by-4-inch labels when the retailer was expecting 6-by-4-inch labels, you'll incur a chargeback. Too many chargebacks will eat away at your profits very quickly.

Chargebacks and other pitfalls aside, with the right wholesale opportunity, your business can take off—and fast. That's what Wallach discovered while exhibiting at the Union Street Fair a few years ago. She stepped up to assist a woman who was examining her handcrafted rings, and was asked whether they could be made into cufflinks. Thinking the woman wanted a pair for her boyfriend, Wallach enthusiastically chirped, "Of course," and then was floored when the customer said she was the California buyer for Nordstrom and was interested in placing an initial order for 400 pairs of cufflinks and 600 necklaces. Eight months later, Wallach's cufflinks, rings, and bracelets were in 17 Nordstrom stores throughout California, and her jewelry empire was born. Also thanks to that chance encounter, Wallach still sells to Nordstrom and to Fred Segal, the trendy California retailer to the stars and the terminally hip. And to illustrate how amazing it is to get such an order, Wallach says that she usually sells 15 and sometimes 30 items at a time to other retailers, so an order for 600 pieces is huge, in more ways than one.

Boutiques and Gift Stores

While every new accessories designer/reseller dreams of landing a big career-making account like Wallach did, they're actually pretty hard to come by. So, instead, you should set your sights on smaller retailers like boutiques and gift stores as outlets for your products. The owners of such stores usually are much more flexible. They buy in much smaller quantities, of course, but they usually are more willing to work with you, they like the exclusivity created by carrying your special brand, and they usually won't kill your profits with endless chargebacks and conditions. In addition, because smaller stores usually are operated by the owner, you'll have the opportunity to develop a warm and friendly relationship with that person, something that goes a long way toward ensuring repeat business down the road.

Donna von Hoesslin, the California belt and jewelry designer, offers another reason why boutiques make better customers for startup businesses. "It's risky to deal with bigger entities like department stores because when they need to cut down inventory, you take a big hit," she says. "I once had an order cancelled midproduction. That kind of thing happens all the time, and it can put you out of business. That's why all my retailers are mom-and-pops, as well as a few small chains. Those relationships are more in-touch relationships and you don't have to worry about chargebacks."

Consignment

Sometimes a retailer isn't ready to commit to a full-scale order for your products but is still interested in offering your merchandise for sale. In that case, you might be offered a consignment arrangement, in which you provide products at no initial cost to the store. The retailer adds the merchandise to her inventory, and when it sells, sends you the proceeds, minus a commission for her trouble. As you can imagine, this isn't the best way to sell accessories because you end up taking all the risk and you tie up valuable inventory with no guarantee of a sale. However, if there's a store you're really desperate to get into, consignment can be the foot in the door you need. Since at this point you're looking for the key to success in marketing your accessories anyway, you might want to try placing some products on consignment to see what happens.

Trade Shows

Here's another way to get your accessories in front of a live, receptive audience with money to spend. There are a number of fashion industry trade shows devoted to accessories alone, as well as several major shows for clothing and accessories, and anyone with the price of a booth space in her marketing budget can be there. In a way, a trade show is a street fair or craft show on steroids. You'll get a huge number of buyers all in one place—often thousands at a time—but they'll be primed to buy rather than just to window shop. Eventually, that is, because although some orders are taken at trade shows, wholesalers often view them simply as a place to generate leads. So make sure you bring tons of business cards. In fact, a box of 500 cards probably won't go to waste.

Smart Tip

Tip...

Always collect a business card from every buyer you talk to when you're working the floor at a trade show. Make notes on the back about which products the buyer was interested in, and when you return to home base, enter the contact and merchandise information into a database so you can follow up with these potential clients later.

Sizing Up the Competition

Whenever possible, you should attend any craft show or street fair you're interested in as a visitor before you commit to exhibiting these in the future. When you're at the show, browse the booths to determine the mix of products, then observe the dynamics on the sales floor or outdoor sales area to see whether people are just browsing or actually buying. Also, chat up the vendors. If they come back to the same show year after year, that means the show has been good for their bottom line—and consequently could give yours a boost, too.

For a comprehensive list of national craft shows, go to artsandcraftshows.net. Another useful resource that can steer you toward potential sales opportunities is the *Sunshine Artist Audit Book,* which is published twice a year and gives information about the thousands of craft and arts shows held across the country. To order a copy, see sunshineartist.com.

Hardy and Howard can attest to the value of doing the trade show circuit. When they first launched their business they learned they had to exhibit at the Southern Clothing Market Trade Show in Charlotte, North Carolina, where the focus is on upscale men's brands. So they acquired a list of key account names from someone in the men's apparel industry who was willing to share, then sent selected retailers an invitation for a private showing of their merchandise before the trade show opened.

Not only did they land six solid appointments with retailers from that mailing, but they left the trade show with 12 retailers on board—a phenomenal response rate for a startup operation.

You'll find a list of some of the largest fashion accessories and fashion trade shows in the Appendix.

Stat Fact

According to post-show buyer research from MAGIC, one of the fashion industry's foremost accessories trade shows, $40 billion in annual consumer sales begins at MAGIC; 90 percent of retailers come to MAGIC looking for new suppliers; 80 percent of buyers purchase at the show; and 93 percent buy as a result of attending.

Sales Representative

You might consider hiring a sales representative who specializes in fashion accessories to hawk your collection. A sales rep handles the product lines of numerous designers and resellers, and calls on store buyers, exhibits at national trade shows, and displays at showrooms as a way to find buyers. However, since they sell in volume, sales reps will *not* represent designers who make one-of-a-kind or custom pieces. Your manufacturing process has to be ramped up to full capacity if you want to work with a sales rep because if you can't meet the quantity requirement of the customer your rep finds, then you don't have a sale.

If you use a sales rep, you still retain control of the wholesale transactions. The rep will fax or e-mail the order to you, and it's up to you to fulfill it. Once you're paid for the merchandise, you pay the rep 15 percent of the order total for her work. That might sound steep, but it's a great way to get your accessories into stores far and wide—places you might never find yourself or have enough time to visit in the course of trying to run a business, design great accessories, and have some semblance of a personal life.

According to handbag designer Brooke Sobel, many people in her industry hire reps to sell for them. Her advice is to find someone who loves your line. You can find such a person through word of mouth among your professional colleagues or sometimes through the Yellow Pages.

Website

These days everyone and his grandmother are online, so it should come as no surprise that the internet is a great place to develop wholesale business. You can do this in one of two ways. You can use your website as an information-only site, as Hardy and Howard do, or you can take orders through it, as David Kulaas, the Colorado scarf designer, does. If you take wholesale orders online, it's crucial that your site is password-protected or otherwise secured so only qualified wholesale buyers can view and purchase merchandise. For instance, Donna von Hoesslin provides serious retail buyers with a special web address so they can browse her merchandise and view the wholesale price. The wholesale site also includes special coding so search engines can't find it.

No matter how you use your site, it's crucial to post the highest quality possible color photos of every item you sell—front and back, if appropriate—since those photos are your personal sales representatives. You'll also want to provide full product information on every item, including details like size or length, color and material. Snappy and evocative copy, like that used on the Southern Proper website at southernproper.com, helps to tell a story and, in the case of these charming Southern-inspired products, weaves a little romance around them.

It's strongly recommended that you make the creation of a website one of the first tasks you undertake when you launch your business. Here's why, according to Hardy of Southern Proper: "Our website gets about 8,000 unique hits per month and helped to create an identity for our brand and spread the word about Southern Proper. Creating a website from the beginning was key to our success and truly got us off the ground and running. The buzz our website created was phenomenal, and without it we would not have experienced the growth we have had."

You'll find information about creating your own website in Chapter 14.

Other Online Opportunities

If you're a handbag designer or reseller, there's one more way to use the internet to make a splash with your high-end merchandise: Contact BagBorrowandSteal.com, which rents upscale and often very expensive designer handbags to its "members" by the week or by the month. For example, a Hermès Vintage Crocodile Piano Handbag rents to members for a cool $442 a week or $1,300 a month, while a Balenciaga pebble grain leather tote in a positively scrumptious shade of red rents for $100 a week, or $295 a month—and there was a waiting list for both at the time this book was written.

Some of the handbags from California designer Brooke Sobel's latest collection are featured on the site, and she says it wasn't all that hard to get them there. "I just kept calling the buyer and sending line sheets, and she saw the line soon after at one of the trade shows," Sobel says. "It was a phenomenal order—10 of each of the bags in my line."

There are other websites that feature high-end handbags for sale, including Zappos.com and Shoes.com. It might be worth contacting them and any others you come across on the internet to see if they'd be interested in buying bags from you.

Your Own Store

Having your own accessories store may seem like a dream come true for an up-and-coming accessories designer/manufacturer/seller. But the truth is it's usually better to start out with one of the other sales channels discussed here before tackling your own store. For one thing, running a store is expensive. You'll have a lot of overhead, including rent (which can be high), utilities, and advertising costs. You'll also drastically reduce your chances of having a personal life since you'll have to spend a lot of time staffing the store. Of course you could hire a few employees, but that's expensive, too, and may be beyond the budget of a startup small-business owner. Finally, you'll

Smart Tip

If you'll be doing business in a city with a big tourist base, like Las Vegas, New Orleans, New York City, or Orlando, your chances of brick-and-mortar retail store success automatically increase. But do the proper due diligence to find the best location. Even tourists with time on their hands won't spend a lot of time chasing after you.

be married to your location by virtue of a long-term lease, and if the location doesn't live up to its promise, you're stuck because it's virtually impossible to break a lease.

Nevertheless, a brick-and-mortar location could be in your future, so the ins and outs are discussed here for your edification.

Shop Talk

Retail experts say that gift shops—the closest thing to an accessories store—can be opened in as little as 600 to 700 square feet. It's recommended that you start small because retail space is leased by the square foot, plus retail experts estimate that it can cost $40,000 and up to prepare your space for occupancy and cover all your other startup expenses. So follow the example of Liza Sonia Wallach, the jewelry designer in California, who leased a 100-square-foot space at a cost of just $4 per square foot, then spent just $2,000 on leasehold improvements. Of course a 100-square-foot space is pretty darn small, but considering that fashion accessories take less room to display and store than other retail products, a space around that size actually may suit your purposes very well, especially when you first launch the business.

Von Hoesslin, the California belt and jewelry designer, started out in her garage, "like everyone else does," she says, before moving into a 600-square-foot building right in the heart of a small, popular beach town. She had been in business for four years at that point but found she needed more room for storing and shipping merchandise. So the front of her facility is used as a showroom/wholesale sales area, while the back is for warehousing and shipping. "It's much smaller than a warehouse, and it has low rent [$500 a month] and not too many lookie-loos," she says.

There are three types of retail environments suitable for an accessories store: a storefront property, a strip mall location, and a mall store. Of course you also can do this startup thing big and move into your own freestanding building, but frankly, you probably won't need that much room and having a huge liability like towering monthly lease payments is akin to startup suicide. Whenever possible, you should strive to keep your startup expenses as low as possible, and becoming a real estate magnate is not a smart way to do that.

Leasing a space is usually preferable to buying when you're starting out. When you're a tenant, you don't have to worry about mundane stuff like fixing the toilet, paying property taxes, and servicing the air conditioning when it conks out on the hottest day of the year. You just call the landlord and let him or her handle the pesky details.

Leasing Basics

When leasing a retail space, it's important to understand all the terms upfront because once you sign on the dotted line, you're committed, and usually for a long period of time. For this reason, it's a good idea to hire an attorney—preferably one with lease experience—to review contracts and other documents before you sign. Some of the terms you need to know are the length of the lease, how the space is measured (some landlords include the thickness of the walls in the measurement, so in effect you're paying for dead space), whether there's an option to renew (so you don't abruptly find yourself out in the street because you didn't agree to new terms), and the cost of the lease.

Typically a lease runs three, five, or ten years. But in general it's a good idea to negotiate a shorter lease with an option to renew, since you don't know how fast your business will grow and what your space needs will be in the future. A shorter lease term gives you more options if you need to move on.

In addition to negotiating the best possible lease, it's crucial to select the best possible location for your new business. Storefront locations in a busy business district (i.e., on Main Street, USA), tourist or resort towns often are ideal locations for a fashion business like yours because you're likely to get foot traffic in addition to drive-bys. Large show windows are a plus because passersby can peek inside and peruse the merchandise in your displays. Just be sure to rotate the merchandise in your window, both to keep the locals interested by showing them something new and exciting, as well as to make sure the sun doesn't fade the merchandise.

Strip mall stores are fairly abundant in most markets and are usually found in very desirable locations at the intersections of major roads. Because they often house basic services like dry cleaners, florists, and restaurants, they are a good place to score some visibility for your business. Strip malls also offer spaces in different sizes so you don't have to take a 5,000-square-foot size suitable for a post office just to get into the location of your choice.

If possible, sign on for a strip mall location that houses other fashion-oriented stores, such as a bridal salon or a shoe store. That way, the people who visit the strip mall are already in a fashion frame of mind and will be more inclined to add nice accessories like jewelry or belts to their clothing purchase. In fact, if you do find yourself next to a bridal salon, for example, you'll want to create fashion accessories just for a bride or her attendants— say, white jewelry to complement a wedding gown or a unique handbag for the bride to carry on her special day.

Mall stores offer high visibility and substantial foot traffic. They also tend to be pretty small when compared to an anchor store— they're frequently less than 1,000 square feet

Beware!
Since there usually are local ordinances concerning the size, shape, placement, and even colors on exterior signs, it's usually best to confer with your landlord to find out what the local rules and restrictions are before you go to the expense of ordering a sign.

each. But in terms of traffic and visibility, a mall store (known as an "inline store" in mall vernacular) can work very well, assuming you have the right mix of stores around you. For instance, if you're selling luxury handbags, you won't want to locate your store in a mall that has big-box retailers like Target or Lowe's, or even department stores like Sears, Mervyn's, or Stein Mart for that matter, because their price points for the same types of merchandise that you offer are likely to be much more moderate, which can kill your sales quickly. On the other hand, a mall with Nordstrom, Macy's, and other high-end retailers will reflect well on your high-end or exclusive merchandise.

Fees and Signage

When you lease a strip mall or mall location, you can expect to pay various marketing and maintenance fees in addition to your monthly lease payment. Maintenance fees can include anything from window washing to store security and trash collection, while marketing fees cover collective holiday marketing efforts and any special advertising done to attract buyers. Storefront leases usually don't have any additional fees tacked on because the building's owner pays property tax that covers street maintenance like snow removal, trash collection, and so on. If you're paying any part of the property tax (likely), it should be included in your lease payment. In any event, be sure you know up front exactly what the extra financial liability is so you don't end up with a payment that's more than your budget can handle comfortably.

Speaking of finances, lease costs vary widely by region. For example, the average price per square foot for retail commercial space in the Puget Sound, Washington, area is $22.40, while lease rates in Orlando, Florida, are $18.10. Compare that with Manhattan, where the average price for ground-floor space is $297 per square foot, and you can see why it's so important to shop around before settling on a location for your store.

Good signage also is a must if you have a storefront or strip mall location. (If your store is in a mall, its management company is likely to take care of your signage.) There are many types of signs to choose from, including hand-painted signs made of vinyl-clad plywood, and channel-letter signs, which consist of hand-painted letters that can be backlit for added impact (the sign used by Off 5th, Saks Fifth Avenue's oh-so-chic clearance outlet, is an example of channel-letter signage). Other common exterior sign styles include backlit electrical signs and

> **Bright Idea**
>
> If you happen to score a much-coveted corner location for your store, be sure to have effective signage created for both the front and the side of the shop so, no matter which way traffic approaches, drivers will be able to see at a glance exactly what you're selling.

▲

Smart Tip

Tip...

Keep your store windows brightly lit at night, both to attract people to look at merchandise and hopefully entice them to return when the store is open, and to deter theft. If a thief has a choice of breaking into a brightly lit store or one that is dark, you can guess which one will be victimized.

dimensional letter/logo signs in materials like metal, plastic, and foam.

Signage costs vary widely, and it's possible to work with a company online to have your sign designed and created. However, it's usually best to find a local company to do the job because you'll want to have installation included as part of the price. Or if you're creative, you can do what Wallach did, and design your own sign. After having her sign project and design approved by the city and the local retail association, she picked up a sheet of plywood from Home Depot and started painting. Recently, however, she decided to have a new sign with an awning made. She was required to obtain detailed architectural drawings to scale before it could be approved. That sign cost $1,200, but Wallach figures it's worth it because it gives her store a more professional appearance.

Store Layout

Because your accessories are the true stars of your retail space, there's no need to design an intricate space with elaborate shelving or themed vignettes. Rather, go for a simple, rectangular box of a shop, then give it lots of design flair by using paint treatments and other decorative touches. You'll need display cases and shelving to showcase the merchandise, as well as some kind of a counter where you will serve customers, approve credit purchases, and wrap merchandise. Just be sure to place your cash/wrap counter near the back of your store. This "forces" customers to walk through your entire store, and often spurs them to make impulse purchases on top of the item they had already planned to buy.

If at all possible, you should include an area (also at the back of the store) for storing extra stock, as well as a small work space for yourself. Alternatively, you can follow Wallach's lead and place a work table right in the shop where customers can watch you make jewelry, design belts, and so on. "You don't have to have a large or fancy store," she says. "My store is so tiny that all the displays consist of jewelry pads nailed vertically to the wall."

At any given time, Wallach has 1,400 jewelry items in the store, including 900 rings. She admits it's a liability that the store is too small for display cases. "I had the money to do the display areas more expensively, but I didn't want to put the cart before the horse," she says. Rather, she preferred to use her startup cash for jewelry materials so she could have the widest selection of products possible.

Of course if you have room for display cases and shelving, you have a lot of options, from traditional display cases for large or more expensive items that you wish to keep under lock and key to Lucite shelves that look like they're floating in air or simple jewelry racks with hooks for hanging long items like necklaces and bracelets. To save some money on retail display items, look in the Yellow Pages under "Store Fixtures" or "Retail Displays" to see if you can find companies that sell second-hand fixtures. You might also try eBay and your local Craigslist.org listings to see if anyone is trying to sell—or give away—store fixtures. If you do find something on eBay, however, be wary of bidding unless you know exactly how much it will cost to ship the item to you—as well as whether shipping is even a possibility. If you're interested in something large and heavy like a display case, it's usually wiser to look for sellers in your immediate area who offer "local pickup only"—assuming, of course, you have a vehicle large enough to haul it away and enough helpers to get it inside.

> **Tip...**
>
> **Smart Tip**
>
> Retail stores that display merchandise like fashion accessories often have closed-in window backs, which block the view into the store. This focuses attention on the merchandise in the showcase rather than on the people inside, and gives you many more options for creating interesting displays.

Other Retail Sales Strategies

There are other ways to sell retail besides going to the major expense and trouble of establishing a brick-and-mortar location. The natural alternative is to sell online through your own website. As with a wholesale-based website, you'll need to describe your accessories fully and show them in great detail as a way to convince surfers to buy. You'll also want to consider trying pay-per-click advertising and other techniques to drive people to your website from a search engine. You'll find more information about how to do this in Chapter 14.

Speaking of online opportunities, you also should consider using an online auction website like eBay to move products. In addition to offering accessories in auction-style listings, you can set up an eBay store to market whatever you're selling. The cost to list products in a store is fairly nominal—3 cents per item, plus a store fee for a 30-day period. If the item(s) doesn't sell, you simply ante up again. Now, if you're an artist and a purist, you might not think that eBay is cool enough to showcase your upscale products in the manner they deserve. However, when you consider that eBay has created a new class of virtual millionaires who sell everything from tsochkes to tanks, then you must agree that eBay deserves a look.

Ditto the home shopping channels like QVC and HSN. It's not as easy to get a product on the shopping networks as it is on eBay—you must audition for a spot, and

Getting Ready for Your Close-Up

Cable shopping networks provide excellent opportunities to be seen and subsequently to sell a ton of merchandise. Here's the 411 on the industry's leading cable shopping networks:

O *QVC.* Before you pitch an item, your product must be in production, or at the very least, you must have a working prototype. The minimum purchase order is usually $30,000 to $35,000 per item at wholesale cost, which equates to a lot of hand-beaded belts or earrings. (Having said that, it's important to note that at the time this book was written QVC was not actively pursuing hand-beaded jewelry items. You'll need to check the company's website frequently to see if that changes.) For more information about the selling and on-air pitching processes, go to qvcproduct search.com.

O *HSN.* This network's minimum inventory amounts are lower than QVC— just $5,000—which is more manageable for a business just starting out. In addition, HSN actively pursues products in all categories at all times, so you can submit an application to audition for a spot selling your fashion accessories at any time. For more details about becoming an HSN partner, go to hsn.com.

you're not assured of getting product placement if you do audition. But as you can imagine, if you crack one of the shopping networks, your fortunes could be made just in terms of sheer volume. However, cable shopping is not for one-of-a-kind products—you have to be mass-producing items to meet the needs of a very large pool of potential buyers. Sometimes it's hard for aspiring entrepreneurs to get enough cash to manufacture massive quantities. So you might want to defer your cable TV debut for a while, or at least until you have a substantial amount of money in the bank or available from a bank or investors.

While you're mulling over those cyber and broadcast options, you might also consider having a trunk show to showcase your accessories. Trunk shows are sales of short duration—sometimes a day or two, sometimes just for a few hours—that are meant to introduce buyers to every product in your current collection. Sometimes retailers who are interested in your accessory line but aren't ready to commit to a purchase will invite you in for such a sale to see how well your collection does. Your hope, of course, is that every last item you bring sells out, which will dazzle the retailer and cause him to instantly place a mammoth order for every other accessory you have in stock. But it's more likely that you will sell a modest number of pieces, which hopefully will be enough to encourage the retailer to place that order.

Just keep in mind that you assume all the risk with a trunk show. The retailer provides nothing except a place to hold it. So to increase the likelihood that your collection will sell, you'll want to promote the heck out of the sale in advance. A well-timed e-mail blast or a direct-mail piece like a brochure sent to prospective customers can go a long way in generating interest and bringing in people.

Alternatively, you can hold your own trunk show, which is an especially good business ploy at the end of the season when you have leftover merchandise to move before your new collection debuts. You can hold your trunk show just about anywhere people congregate, but one of the best places is a hotel suite or banquet room because it's a cost-effective option that gives you plenty of room to display your merchandise. Limit the trunk show to no more than about three to four hours and offer refreshments to those who come in to browse. Also be sure to have wireless point-of-sale equipment on hand (discussed in Chapter 8) to process charge sales, as well as materials to package purchases.

Hardy and Howard, the Georgia men's accessories wholesalers, have had a lot of success with trunk shows. In one case, they sent 500 invitations to investment bankers, attorneys, and other business professionals who buy ties, and invited them to a cocktail event where they showed their merchandise. The event was a big hit and resulted in many new sales.

One final retail option is to stage a home party in the style of Longaberger, the handcrafted basket manufacturer, or Mary Kay Cosmetics. After finding a friend or business colleague to host the party, invite people to come to view your collection over a glass of wine, perhaps, and hors d'oeuvres. It's not necessary to bring enough products with you to fulfill orders—rather, you simply bring a sample of everything in your collection, then take orders that can be fulfilled at a later date. It's a great way to acquaint a roomful of people with your accessories, as well as to start building a loyal fan base for future collections. Naturally, in addition to covering the food and drinks, you'll want to give the host an item from your collection as a thank you for so graciously opening his or her home for the party.

Fulfilling Orders

No discussion of sales channels would be complete without information about fulfillment, which is the process of taking orders, then packaging and shipping the merchandise to your customers. When you start your business, you'll probably be able to handle the fulfillment yourself. But when your e-commerce venture grows to the point that you're spending too much time on nonrevenue-generating activities, then it's time either to hire some people to help or to outsource the order fulfillment process.

Hiring people is always a huge step in a new business's life cycle. It's also one that should be deferred as long as possible because, to be perfectly frank, employees are *ver-rrrry* expensive. One way to dodge some of the debt is to use independent contractors, but as you might expect, the IRS has pretty strict ideas about who can be considered a contractor and who's really an employee. You'll find a detailed discussion of employees and other helpers in the next chapter.

Another way to make sure your valued customers get the merchandise they order in a timely fashion is to hire an order fulfillment company. As you can imagine, this can be pretty pricey, too, but you can certainly pass along the handling charges to your customers (that's the "h" in "shipping and handling" charges).

You can find order fulfillment houses pretty much in every major city in the country. Some things to keep in mind when hiring one are:

- *Location.* Pick one that's close to your customers, not your own location. For example, let's say you're doing business in California but most of your customers are located on the East Coast. You'll want to warehouse your merchandise at a fulfillment house somewhere in the middle of the country or even toward the east so shipping charges will be lower.

- *Size.* You need a fulfillment service that can meet your daily order fulfillment needs, no matter how much they fluctuate. Ask how spikes in orders are handled.

- *Shipping options.* You'll want to select a fulfillment center that offers many shipping options so you can accommodate most customers' needs.

- *Turnaround time.* This becomes especially important around heavy gift-giving occasions, like the December holidays and Mother's Day. Make sure you know exactly when orders have to be received (i.e., at what time of the day) to meet next-day or two-day shipping processing deadlines.

- *Error rate.* Everyone makes mistakes, so it's important to know how the fulfillment house rectifies them. Find out how it handles situations where the customer receives the wrong information or a product is shipped to the wrong place.

- *Cost.* This is a biggie. Depending on the fulfillment house, you may pay a per-order or per-item fee, a base fee to store inventory, and/or a pallet fee. Be sure you're clear about all the charges before you send a single accessory there.

There's one last way to fulfill orders if you'll be operating as a reseller—and you never have to touch a single product. Some manufacturers offer drop-shipping, which is a process by which you take orders, forward them to the manufacturer, and sit back while the factory handles the fulfillment. As a drop-shipper, you'll earn just a percentage of the wholesale price as your payment, but when you consider that you have no upfront costs, no inventory, no warehousing issues and no employees, it can be a pretty good deal. So when you're out and about looking for manufacturers, put a question about drop-shipping on your master list of inquiries. It can be a great way to make a few extra bucks with virtually no financial liabilities.

For more information on starting a retail store, check out Entrepreneur's *Start Your Own Retail Store*.

Friends
of Fashion:
Your Employees

Owning and operating a business is exciting and exhilarating—and a lot of work. There will be days that you think you can't possibly do one more thing, then somehow, you'll find an extra reserve of strength into which you can tap to get the job done.

Of course even with that wellspring of strength and adrenaline, there still are only 24 hours in a day. If a significant number of those hours include time spent in a retail store selling accessories, then the amount of time you have for other projects (like designing product lines, balancing the books, purchasing inventory, and so on) will be drastically reduced. That's why it was recommended in Chapter 7 that you turn over some business functions to a reliable bookkeeper or accountant and a computer guru. But the day will come when you'll need help running your store or keeping up with the paperwork involved with operating the business—and that day could come sooner than later, depending upon the success of your business.

Even so, most small-business experts recommend deferring the decision to hire as long as possible. After all, in the startup phase of any business, you can't always be certain about the reliability of your revenue stream. But employees still have to be paid whether business is good or bad, and the added stress of worrying about meeting payroll is a hassle you don't need.

Nevertheless, if you do think you'll need help, you should plan for that contingency when you are putting together your startup budget. Simply include the cost of six months' worth of salaries and taxes (or hourly contractor wages) for each employee in your projections. That will be enough cash to get the business up and running, and hopefully will give you enough time to start making money.

If you'll be a brick-and-mortar retail store owner, you'll most likely need retail clerks. Virtual retailers may need a clerical assistant and/or fulfillment clerk to help box up and ship orders, as well as someone to process orders taken off your website, write copy for new products and post it to the website. A designer/manufacturer may need a clerical assistant, a designer or a pattern maker. This chapter covers the basics of finding those employees and figuring out what to do with them when you do have them.

Finding Good Help

Small-business owners everywhere say that finding and keeping reliable employees is among the toughest tasks as an employer. For one thing, it seems like employees with good customer service skills have gone the way of the dodo, no doubt because of the anonymous and touchless environment of the internet, which has diminished their people skills. In addition, young people, who traditionally fill lower paying retail and clerical jobs, seem to be more interested in their iPods and iPhones than in making a few bucks, and may not even have to work, thanks to the generosity of their two-income parents.

That said, it's really important to find good employees because it takes both time and money away from your company when you have to keep training new people. The best place to start looking for help is among your own family members, friends, and business associates, who might either be looking for a job themselves or can recommend someone qualified for the job. Alternatively, you can either advertise for help in the local paper or on an online job board like Monster .com. You also can contact your local college or university to find students who might be interested in an internship with your company. It's actually quite common in the fashion industry to use unpaid interns, who are more interested in obtaining experience and job skills than in a paycheck. However, entrepreneurs like Reagan Hardy and Emmie Howard, co-owners of Southern Proper in Georgia, believe it's important to pay interns for their contributions.

> ### Smart Tip Tip...
>
> A prospective employee who comes to you on the recommendation of a friend, family member, or acquaintance often is a much better candidate than someone off the street who merely answers a classified ad. Presumably, your personal network will only recommend truly qualified and reliable prospects, so all you have to do is determine whether your personalities mesh well.

"Our interns are not just answering e-mails or answering the phone," says Howard. "They're working alongside me and Reagan and doing key jobs like building relationships with our customers and working on the product development and marketing side of the business. They are a huge help to us, and we reward them for their hard work and dedication by paying them a stipend."

Not that young people are your only prospects. Baby boomers are a gold mine of talent because they're often looking for something to keep themselves busy after retirement. So are stay-at-home moms, who may need a part-time source of income.

> ### Bright Idea
>
> If you need help with a short-term project, like shipping out packages or mailing line sheets to wholesale customers, call a temporary employment agency. Temps come to you pre-screened for the job and ready to work, and when the work is done, they're done, too—until the next time you need to call in temporary reinforcements.

Screening and Hiring Procedures

Once you have a potential pool of candidates, review their resumes carefully. While retail or fashion experience is important, so is reliability (apparent from a history of continued and continuous employment) and a background in customer service (the field doesn't matter as much as the skills do). Be sure to write a job description before you interview anyone so you can communicate the exact scope of the job. Then when you invite candidates in for an interview, have them fill out a job application before you talk. Although you can create a customized application, you'll find it's easier just to pick up a pack of blank job applications from an office supply store.

During the interview, talk to the candidate candidly, and spend an equal amount of time just listening. You'll get a good idea about the temperament and enthusiasm of a candidate by the way he or she interacts with you. Take note, too, of nonverbal cues. Someone who smiles, looks friendly, and seems interested in what you have to say is probably a good candidate.

In fact, good chemistry is really important, almost more important than job experience. You'll be working closely with your employee every day, so find someone you like and who has values similar to your own for the best chance of having a harmonious working relationship.

You don't have to discuss specifics like salary, commission or benefits at the interview, even if the candidate asks about them. You should table that discussion until you're ready to make an offer, since the point of meeting prospects is to find someone who's a good fit. The financial details can be worked out later.

Setting Wages

Salaries and per-hour pay are often determined by the local market. According to CareerBuilder.com's website at cbsalary.com, the U.S. national average salary for a full-time retail sales clerk is $21,923, which works out to just over $10.42 per hour based on a 40-hour week, or around $1,806 per month. That might sound high, especially if you live in a state like Wyoming, where the minimum wage is $5.15 per hour. By comparison, the minimum wage is $8 an hour in Massachusetts and $7.15 an hour in New York. Obviously, someone is paying his or her employees much more than minimum wage if the average is so high, which you might need to do, too, to attract high-caliber employees. You can find a list of minimum wages by state on the U.S. Department of Labor's website at dol.gov.

Here's another way to figure out a reasonable salary: Use a salary search engine like cbsalary.com or indeed.com, which allow you to plug in both the city and title of the job you're interested in. At the time this book was written, cbsalary.com said that the U.S. national average salary for a retail sales clerk was $21,923. Naturally, the average salary in your area might be higher or lower depending upon the strength of the local economy. 125

By the way, cbsalary.com says that the national average salary for a general office clerk is $23,020. If you'd like to know what the average wage is for your metro area, try plugging in the search term "general office clerk" and your ZIP code in the salary search box on indeed.com.

When you're working on a low startup budget, these salary figures might freak you out. But just remember that you're more likely to need part-time than full-time help at first, so you can automatically cut those proposed salary figures by 40 to 50 percent.

Benefits

While benefits are greatly appreciated by employees, it's actually quite common for small-business owners to offer just a salary and/or a commission to new hires. It's not hard to figure out why. A recent U.S. Chamber of Commerce study indicated that benefits account for 40 percent of payroll expenses, which usually is a budget-buster for a small business. So if you would like to do something extra for a hard-working employee, you might offer a week of paid vacation or a couple of personal days instead as a way to keep job satisfaction and morale high.

Taxes

Here's another reason why many small-business owners decide to go it alone at first. When you take on an employee, you have to collect taxes on his or her wages, plus pay a whole bunch of business taxes. Employee taxes include federal, state, and possibly local income tax, FICA (aka Social Security), and Medicare, all of which must be collected from the employee's wages and sent in to the IRS on a quarterly basis. If you're operating as a sole proprietor, you have to send in quarterly taxes on your own wages, too.

Then as an employer, you'll pay:

- The matching portion of the FICA, or Social Security tax, which in 2008 was 6.2 percent
- The matching portion of Medicare taxes (1.45 percent)
- State unemployment tax (the amount varies by state)
- Self-employment tax on your own earnings if you're a sole proprietor (which is the other half of the Social Security tax on your personal earnings since you're self-employed)
- Federal Unemployment Tax (FUTA), which pays for unemployment insurance programs (another 6.2 percent, or just .8 percent if you pay state unemployment insurance)
- Workers' compensation insurance (which varies by state)

As you can imagine, it takes time to keep all these payments and requirements straight. If you're so inclined, you can use software like Intuit QuickBooks's enhanced

> ## Bright Idea
> An easy way to file federal employee tax payments for both yourself and your employees is by using EFTPS-Direct, the federal government's free electronic tax payment system. You can pay by check over the internet using your employer identification number or Social Security number. For more information or to enroll, log onto eftps.gov or call (800) 555-8778.

▲

payroll and tax filing add-on ($200 a year) to handle the details (go to pay roll.intuit.com for more information), or you can turn over the job to your bookkeeper. Unless you really enjoy crunching numbers, you'll probably be happier giving the responsibility for tax collection to someone else. But if you want further information about withholding and taxes before making a decision, pick up a copy of IRS Publication 15, *Employer's Tax Guide*; and Publication 583, *Starting a Business and Keeping Records*. Both are available online from irs.gov or at your local IRS office.

Independent Contractors

If your eyes glazed over with all this talk about hiring and taxes, then take heart—independent contractors can be a viable alternative to regular employees. You usually have to pay contractors a little more per hour than the average employee. But in the long run, they're much more cost-effective because you don't have to worry about FICA and other employment taxes. Instead, you report contractor income over $600 on a 1099-MISC form at the end of the tax year, and the contractor is responsible for handling the taxes herself.

I.D., Please

If you're planning to bring employees aboard to help you steer your fledgling fashion accessories ship, you'll be required to have an employer identi-fication number (EIN). Issued free of charge by the IRS, the EIN is a nine-digit num-ber used to identify the tax accounts of business entities that have employees (including sole proprietors), are organized as a corporation or a partnership, or meet certain other criteria. It replaces your Social Security number (SSN) on any IRS correspondence, but only related to your business. You'll continue to use your SSN on personal tax returns and other official documents.

Applying for an EIN is simple. Simply go to irs.gov and fill out the online EIN application. Once the application is completed and validated, you'll receive your EIN immediately. You also can apply by phone and receive an EIN right away by calling the Business & Specialty Tax Line at (800) 829-4933 during normal busi-ness hours. Finally, you can apply by mail by filling out form SS-4, which is avail-able at irs.gov, but it will take four weeks for the application to be processed.

Since it's sometimes necessary to have an EIN when you open a business bank account, apply for a business license or file any type of business tax return by mail, you should apply for yours immediately. For more information about EINs, visit the IRS website.

Of course nothing is that simple when it comes to dear old Uncle Sam. Here's what your favorite relative has to say about independent contractors: "The general rule is that an individual is an independent contractor if you, the person for whom the services are performed, have the right to control or direct *only the result of the work* and not the means and methods of accomplishing the result." What that means is that you can assign the work, but the contractor is free to complete it any way she wishes. In addition, the IRS usually considers someone who works onsite in your place of business, even if that place is your home, to be an employee rather than an independent contractor. That, of course, can be a problem if you want the contractor to work in your store or in your home. Finally, contractors are supposed to be paid by the job rather than by the hour (although you can base the per-job rate on the number of hours worked).

> **⚠ Beware!**
> It's usually best to use independent contractors for work that isn't sensitive or confidential, like office administration or product fulfillment. If a contractor will have access to your confidential designs, have him sign a confidentiality agreement promising not to divulge details about them to anyone. Your attorney can draw up a simple agreement for you to use.

As you can tell, the contractor-employee relationship is complicated. To make sure you don't run afoul of the IRS, talk to your accountant or bookkeeper about your options if you use independent contractors. In the meantime, if you'd like further information about what constitutes the employer-employee vs. contractor relationship, pick up a copy of IRS Publication 15-A, *Employer's Supplemental Tax Guide*, available online (irs.gov) or at your local IRS field office.

Because there are no fashion industry guidelines about how much an independent contractor should be paid, you can set the rate wherever you wish—although do expect the contractor to have something to say about it. You can use the salary figures mentioned earlier as a starting point.

Professional Development

If you've passed over the magic threshold into adulthood, then you know it's possible to get a good job—or in this case, to start a business—without a formal or specialized education. But you probably also know that education makes the process of making a living much easier. Besides broadening your horizons, education gives you options and makes you a more informed and insightful thinker. For this reason, we recommend that you learn as much as possible about the fashion industry because:

- Staying abreast of the changes in this volatile field will help you make better merchandising choices.
- Understanding how the industry works will make it easier to find products, services, and other resources you need.
- Being familiar with good business practices will keep you from making costly mistakes you could have avoided.

Now you definitely can pay someone to be your eyes and ears in the industry. But not only is that a costly way to do business, it's not much fun, either. So if you really want to enjoy your new profession, take the time to get acquainted with the industry by using its many professional development tools, including industry associations, publications, and even academic programs leading to fashion design and business management degrees.

Fashion Industry Associations

For an industry that is so diverse, there are surprisingly few fashion associations—at least those that are open to aspiring entrepreneurs. (For example, the Council of Fashion Designers of America caters to the industry's foremost fashion and accessories designers, and membership is by invitation only.)

- One of the biggest and best-known associations is the *American Apparel and Footwear Association*, a national organization for apparel, footwear, and sewn products companies and their suppliers. It's of limited value to accessories business owners other than for information about the industry, plus dues start at $2,500 a year. For more information, see apparelandfootwear.org.
- The only association devoted entirely to fashion accessories is the *Accessories Council* (accessoriescouncil.org), a national advocacy organization dedicated to increasing consumer awareness of and demand for fashion accessories. It offers networking, educational, and marketing opportunities, members-only discounts and more. Companies with sales under $2 million pay a membership fee of $510 annually.
- The *Color Association of the United States* (colorassociation.com) predicts color trends and seasonal palettes, and you have to be a member to get the 411 on what's new and exciting in color, color education, and research. Annual membership costs $600, plus a $300 registration fee for new members.
- The *Fashion Accessories Shippers' Association* (geminishippers.com) might be a useful organization to join if you're planning to import products. Also known as the National Fashion Accessories Association, this nonprofit trade association offers cost-effective logistics for international importing and exporting, updated international trade information, advice on legal and governmental

affairs, and information about U.S. customs regulations. There is no charge to join.

- The nonprofit *Fashion Group International* (fgi.org) counts apparel, accessories, beauty, and home companies among its members. It offers information about contemporary trend and business information, industry sources, market data, educational seminars, and more. It also publishes trend reports, newsletters featuring industry reports and business insights, and an annual membership directory. Now here's the catch: To become an associate member, you must have at least one year of experience in a fashion-related industry, so this is an organization to which you can aspire down the road. The dues you pay depend on where you do business. For example, the dues in Illinois are $70, plus a $25 initiation fee, while in New York, the dues are $100 plus a $25 initiation fee.

- The *Fashion Jewelry Trade Association* (fjta.org) is devoted to protecting the interests of fashion jewelry suppliers and retailers through lobbying and other coordinated efforts. At $1,500 for annual dues (plus a $3,000 initiation fee—ouch) this is another one of those organizations to aspire to, but you can find a lot of free information on its website in the meantime.

- The *International Jewelry Designer's Guild* (jewelrydesignersguild.com) is an online community and support group for jewelry artists and artisans. Membership is free for qualified jewelry designers.

- *Wholesalecrafts.com* (wholesalecrafts.com), though not an association per se, is an organization for artist-owned studios. Its chief benefit is as a place to advertise affordably, and its website offers a plethora of resources for artists and designers seeking retail outlets for their products.

> ## Bright Idea
>
> If you want a really current snapshot of what people are thinking and saying about fashion trends, hot products, and more, read a fashion blog. Among the well-known fashion-forward publications that have their own blogs are *New York Magazine, Glamour, Teen Vogue, In Style* (which recently had an "In Your Bag" blog), and *The New York Times* fashion section.

Industry Websites of Interest

- *American Gem Society (ags.org)*. A consumer site with useful general information.
- *The Fashion Center (fashioncenter.com)*. An online directory with industry links and fashion information.
- *Handbag Designer 101 (handbagdesigner101.com)*. Information about bag trends, celebrity bags, handbag events and bag forums.
- *Intergem (intergem.com)*. An international gem and jewelry show website.

- *Jewelry and Retail Industry Guide (smadesigngroup.com)*. Links to many industry sites.
- *Pantone.com (pantone.com)*. An authority on color and maker of those skinny color strip books with every color known to (wo)man that artists use when planning product design and print jobs.
- *Style.com (style.com)*. The online home of *Vogue* magazine, with fashion, news, trend information, and much more (could be considered a guilty pleasure until you remember how important it is to stay up to date on what's new and exciting in the fashion industry—so enjoy).
- *Women's Jewelry Association (womensjewelry.org)*. Information about jewelry design, fashion trends, and industry advice.

Trade/Project Publications

Another easy way to stay current on news, information, events, and trends in the fashion and fashion accessories industries is by subscribing to publications that serve not only fashion accessories designers/retailers/wholesalers but also business owners in general. Trade publications you might find useful include.

- *Accessories magazine (accessoriesmagazine.com)*. Covers jewelry, leather, handbags, sunglasses, belts, and more for the retailer and manufacturer; regular coverage of timely fashion trends, plus statistics, retail profiles, consumer surveys, merchandising and display tips and more; ten issues, $43.75—with a catch: the publication must be delivered to a business address.
- *Bead Style (beadstylemag.com)*. Projects, time-saving tips, and more; six issues, $22.95.
- *Beadwork (interweave.com/bead)*. A source of inspiration, free projects, and more; six issues, $19.95.
- *California Apparel News*. You don't have to be on the west coast to find this weekly tabloid publication useful. A subscription is $89 at accessoryweb.com (then click on *Apparel News*). The online edition, ApparelNews.net, is $99, or you can have both for $139/year. This publication frequently shows up at trade shows, so you can preview a copy there if you're not ready to buy.
- *Fashion Accessories and Supplies magazine (netmagazines.com)*. Published for executives in the fashion jewelry, watch, boutique, gift, and related industries; contains articles on current and advance seasonal fashions, equipment, processes, and more; two years (24 issues), $42.
- *Global Sources Fashion Accessories Magazine (globalsources.com)*. Overviews of new products, sourcing reports, supplier information, and more related to sourcing

around the world; includes special editorial sections and advertising on accessories, bags, footwear, and jewelry; $75 for 12 issues.

- *Jewelry Artist magazine (lapidaryjournal.com)*. Articles on gemstones and bead and jewelry arts; also has step-by-step jewelry-making tutorials; 12 issues, $29.95.

- *Stores* magazine *(nrf.com)*. A publication of the National Retail Federation, *Stores* is included with an annual membership to this organization ($175 annually for retailers with a total sales volume under $1 million). It's useful for its in-depth articles on all aspects of the retail industry, retail sales outlook reports, custom databases, research, conferences, and more.

- *Women's Wear Daily (wwd.com)*. Written for both retailers and manufacturers of women's apparel, accessories, fibers, and textiles, this daily newspaper is considered the bible of the retail fashion world. Subscriptions are $169 for 250 issues and several special fashion supplements.

SCOREing Some Help

If you're like many entrepreneurs, you have a lot of enthusiasm for and knowledge about your product(s), but you may lack the hard business management skills needed to handle day-to-day operations. You definitely should consider signing up for those university and adult education courses mentioned in this chapter, but if you need quick startup help, consider contacting SCORE.

SCORE is a nonprofit, nationwide network of retired and working volunteers, entrepreneurs, and corporate managers/executives. This resource partner of the SBA is known as the "Counselors to America's Small Business," and since its founding in 1964, has helped 8 million small businesses with the formation, growth, and success of their operations.

SCORE counselors provide free, confidential small-business advice and mentoring during face-to-face counseling sessions at 389 chapter offices nationwide. The organization also offers low-cost business workshops, online learning, business tools and templates on its website at score.org, and two free e-newsletters, *SCORE eNews* and *SCORE Expert Answers eNewsletter*.

To tap into this awesome resource, visit the SCORE website or call (800) 634-0245.

Consumer Publications

Informed business owners read what their customers read, so here's a list of some of the fashion industry's most influential publications:

- *Cosmopolitan (cosmopolitan.com)*. Considered the authority on fashion trends; 12 issues, $18.
- *Elle (elle.com)*. Focuses on women's fashion, beauty, health, and entertainment; 12 issues, $10.
- *Glamour (glamour.com)*. Every woman's fashion and beauty bible—until about the age of 40; 12 issues, $12.
- *InStyle (instyle.com)*. Lots of fashion news from celebrity style makers; 12 issues for the puzzling price of $23.88.
- *Marie Claire (marieclaire.com)*. Covers fashion, style, beauty, and more; 12 issues, $8.
- *Vogue (style.com/vogue)*. Fashion and lifestyle magazine with insider news, designer interviews, catwalk shots, photo galleries, and calendar of upcoming fashion events; 12 issues, $15.

> **Fun Fact**
>
> The character of Miranda Priestly in the film *The Devil Wears Prada* allegedly was modeled on London-born Anna Wintour, editor in chief of American *Vogue* since 1998. She attended the press screening for the film dressed from head-to-toe in Prada.

Broadcast/Streaming Resources

No one has launched a fashion channel or show dedicated to accessories—yet—but here are a few general fashion channels that are worth a look.

- *Fashion TV (style.com/vogue)*. Fashion, beauty, and style network on cable and satellite networks 24/7.
- *Style Network (mystyle.com)*. All the style you can handle, delivered 24/7 by your cable or satellite TV provider.
- *Vogue.tv (vogue.tv)*. The best of the magazine delivered to your desktop.

Education

Educational opportunities abound in the fashion industry. There are academic programs available to help you become a designer, learn about textiles, understand visual merchandising techniques, and so on.

> **Fun Fact**
>
> Parsons The New School for Design (as it was renamed in 2005) of New York City was founded in 1896 as the Chase School, and offered the country's first program in fashion design in 1906. Among its famous alumni are Donna Karan, Narciso Rodriguez, and Tom Ford.

Typical degrees in this industry include associate and bachelor's degrees in fashion design, retail management, marketing, and merchandising. In addition, you can take a specialized course of study that doesn't lead to a degree but provides you with invaluable insider information about the industry and the tools that will make you a more savvy business owner.

For a comprehensive list of schools nationwide that offer fashion degrees, visit fashionschools.org. Some of the schools offer distance-learning opportunities (usually online), so you can learn wherever you live or work.

Smart Tip

Tip...

It may be possible to claim a tuition and fee deduction on your tax return of up to $4,000 for qualified higher education expenses. Naturally the IRS has a lot of conditions attached to the deduction, so refer to IRS Publication 970, *Tax Benefits for Education,* for the skinny on what qualifies.

Academic education is especially helpful when you're ready to expand your business or your horizons. In the meantime, though, don't overlook the importance of basic business classes that can help you become a more knowledgeable and informed business owner. If you haven't previously had any courses in or don't have any experience with finance, marketing, advertising, information technology, or the many other disciplines you need to master to be a successful business owner, you might want to look into the offerings of your local community college or adult education program to fill in those knowledge gaps. The goal isn't to become a master at balancing the books or troubleshooting computer problems; you just need to know enough to keep the business humming along and tell any professionals you *do* hire just how to proceed. In addition, having at least a rudimentary business background will help you actually understand what your hired guns have to say and how to make the most of their advice.

13

Making an
Advertising
Splash

So you've got these great products that you've designed or carefully selected. They're in stock and priced right. All you need to do now is start shipping them to eager customers. But you need a way to find those customers and induce them to beat a path to your cyber or brick-and-mortar door. The way to make that happen, of course, is by advertising.

▲

Now, when you think of advertising, you probably automatically think of the "big boys"—the Allstates and Coca Colas and FreeCreditReport.coms of the world. But don't even go there. You can't afford advertising on *that* level. (Case in point: The average cost of a 30-second spot aired during Super Bowl XLII in 2008 was a cool $2.7 million—which we feel safe in assuming is just a tad outside your startup budget.) But the fact is, there are a lot of things you can do to spread the word about your product lines that won't bankrupt you—and that, in fact, can put your company squarely on the path to success.

Fashion accessories business owners tend to use just a few advertising tools, including line sheets and print ads. We'll address these in this chapter, as well as present a few others for your consideration that, assuming you have the time and the budget, you may wish to try in your quest to start spreading the news about your products. In addition, internet advertising strategies are discussed in Chapter 14.

Your Marketing Plan

Before you start writing checks to advertisers, you need to write a marketing plan. According to the SBA, "A sound marketing plan is key to the success of your business. It should include your market research, location, the customer group you have targeted,

---

Building a Brand

One of the things that should definitely be included in your marketing plan is a branding strategy. Branding refers to the distinctive characteristics of your company that make it what it is. A logo (or symbol representing your company, like Ford Motor Company's blue oval) is part of the branding process, as is anything you do that sets your business apart from the competition. For example, California entrepreneur Donna von Hoesslin's branding strategy for her line of surfer-inspired belts and jewelry is that everything is handmade, ethically made, and sweatshop free. She also donates 1 percent of her sales to environmental causes. This branding strategy reflects both her business and personal philosophy, and sets her apart from others in the same market.

So your task is to find a way to build a brand strategy that focuses on the benefits, advantages, and uniqueness of your product(s), then communicate it to your valued customers.

---

competition, positioning, the product or service you are selling, pricing, advertising, and promotion." Now, if you did your market research homework as described in Chapter 5, you'll find that you already have some of this information right at hand. Your next step is to create a document that neatly encapsulates this information so it can be used as a road map to keep your business on track and your marketing dollars working effectively.

The marketing plan is often included as part of a company's business plan, and it should be updated periodically—say, annually—or at least when market conditions change so you are always in touch with the needs of your customers. (Remember those lariat necklaces we mentioned in Chapter 5? Devising a new strategy for clearing them out when the market cools is the type of information you'd include when you update your marketing plan.)

SWOT Analysis

Another thing you need to do to prepare yourself and your business to enter the advertising market is to create a business tool known as a SWOT analysis. SWOT stands for:

- *Strengths:* These are characteristics that make you special and set you apart from the competition.
- *Weaknesses.* These are things you need to overcome or work on that your competitors could take advantage of.
- *Opportunities.* This includes anything you can do that might benefit your business either now or in the future.
- *Threats.* Here you identify things that can harm your business.

By thinking through these opportunities and challenges, you'll find yourself in a better position to understand your market and what you need to do to make your business successful.

The following is an example of what a SWOT analysis might look like for a virtual fashion accessories business that sells handbags wholesale. You'll notice that it's very personal—it uses first-person language to make it more immediate and viable to the person who writes it.

Strengths

- My strong business background (glad I got that business degree!).
- My five years of retail sales experience at Sears, which will come in handy when making sales calls.
- My strong communication skills (especially writing).

Weaknesses

- I'm actually a little shy—might be difficult putting myself on the line at first during sales calls.

- I have zero experience with advertising, marketing.
- I can't make out-of-town sales calls when the kids are out of school because it's hard to find short-term day care.

Opportunities

- No one sells handbags even remotely like mine.
- A friend of a friend knows [insert actress name here] and might be able to give a handbag directly to her (excellent photo op possibility!).
- Handbags are manufactured by a company with a small carbon footprint, a fact I can use in advertising to earth-conscious consumers.

Threats

- My per-bag cost is a little high—maybe too high for an untried product (need to look into cost-cutting measures that won't compromise quality).
- Knock-offs are rampant in the fashion industry and can kill my business—need to trademark my product right away.

Here's what a SWOT analysis might look like for a brick-and-mortar accessories store:

Strengths

- Did merchandising work in college, so I know how to set up dynamite displays on a budget.
- Four years' experience selling fine jewelry at Saks.
- Main Street location in a chic resort town.

Weaknesses

- Somewhat undercapitalized—might be strapped for cash when buying for next season; might have to tap the family wealth (such as it is).
- Must limit store hours because no budget for employees right now.

Opportunities

- Location on Main Street between a shoe store and a bridal salon—might be able to work out reciprocal advertising opportunities.
- Plan to start gift certificate program in advance of the holidays.
- Can design jewelry in the front window when the store is quiet to help keep up with orders and attract passersby.

Threats

- Tourism is down because of high gas prices and slowdown in local economy (worrisome number of foreclosures).
- Lots of very young teens in the immediate area who probably will just window shop.

SWOT Analysis Worksheet

Do a SWOT analysis for your own business.

Strengths

1. _____
2. _____
3. _____

Weaknesses

1. _____
2. _____
3. _____

Opportunities

1. _____
2. _____
3. _____

Threats

1. _____
2. _____
3. _____

Try creating your own SWOT analysis using the blank form we've provided above. You can also use the SWOT approach to analyze the strengths and weaknesses of your competition to see how you compare. Then be sure to keep your SWOT analysis handy—it's a great tool to help you judge how well you're addressing your weaknesses and whether you're making progress toward achieving your goals.

▲

Calling Card

Every fashion accessories entrepreneur needs business cards—and for the size, they pack a lot of punch. Naturally, if you're a wholesaler you will want to give your card out judiciously (i.e., to prospects). But if you're in the retail trade, hand your card out everywhere you go, including the post office, the grocery store, the dog groomer, and so on. When you pass along your card this way, you're recruiting every person you meet to be an accessories ambassador. You can't beat that kind of exposure, especially since people tend to file away business cards or pass them along when they encounter someone who needs whatever you're selling.

Always have your business cards professionally printed. It's tempting to buy a package of blank Avery business cards at the office superstore and print them yourself as a way to save money, but if you're selling upscale fashion accessories, you need an upscale look. Even the most expensive business cards will only cost about $50 to $75 for a box of 1,000 at the office superstores, so don't overlook this opportunity to make a professional impression.

Advertising Strategies

Now that your marketing plan is good to go, you can start planning some well-targeted, cost-effective advertising strategies to bring your products to the attention of your soon-to-be-adoring public. Here's the skinny on commonly used techniques that you may wish to try.

Line Sheets

These tools are not just a little something to try on the way to Accessory Stardom—if you sell wholesale, they're integral to the success of your business. Strictly speaking, line sheets are not advertising pieces in the same way a direct mailer or a brochure is. Rather, they're like a streamlined product catalog—so streamlined that they might

Smart Tip

Tip...

Line sheets should always be accompanied by an order form, which you can have printed at the same time your line sheets are printed. If you're using Microsoft Office, you can select from a variety of customizable sales order forms on the Microsoft website at office .microsoft.com. You'll find a sample sales order form from the site reproduced on page 152.

Bright Idea

If you offer the same item in more than one color, you might want to include printed "color swatches" on your line sheet so your prospect doesn't have to imagine what "Banner Blue" or "Kiss Me Pink" look like. (Especially important for male customers, unless your line includes colors like "Vikings Purple" or "Red Wings Scarlet.")

consist of only a single page or just a few pages.

Line sheets depict all the items in your product line or collection, along with product names, item numbers, and simple sketches (see samples on page 149). If you have the budget you may wish to have professional photos taken of each product instead, but beware: Professional photography is expensive, which is why even big companies go for simple pen and ink sketches. These drawings or photos are accompanied by brief product descriptions, item numbers and names, and wholesale prices.

Your line sheet also should include other pertinent information like season, fabric or material information, delivery dates and order minimums, and full contact information, including website, e-mail addresses, and business and/or cell numbers.

You'll use your line sheets a lot, from handing them to prospective retail buyers (e.g., store owners) when you call on them in person to mailing them to prospects who inquire about your product line(s). To keep up with the demand, you can print them yourself on your home color printer (but only if the printing quality is high and you use a good quality paper), or you can upload a file of your sheet(s) to the website of a printer or an office superstore like OfficeMax and have the store output your line sheets in color on high quality paper.

Once your line sheets are printed and ready to go, protect them like gold. Industry insiders admit that there's a lot of espionage in the fashion industry, so if you don't want to see knock-offs of your new and existing products before you have a chance to market them yourself, be very careful to whom you give line sheets.

Smart Tip

Tip...

Make sure your line sheets have a consistent overall look for easy readability. For example, if your summer items are boxed with details below them, make sure winter products are laid out the same way. Also, keep the top left corner of the page blank in case the pages are stapled together. That way important information won't be inadvertently obscured.

Print Ads

In the pantheon of media promotion, print ads are one of the more cost-effective media available to small-business owners. However, "cost-effective" is a relative term—while newspaper and magazine advertising is cheaper than TV or cable

Bright Idea

There are quite a few books available to help you write a marketing plan, including *Entrepreneur's Marketing Made Easy.* You can also find a lot of useful (and free) how-to information on the SBA's website at sba.gov.

advertising, it can still be pretty expensive. One reason is because it's not enough to run an ad once or even twice. You need to run it repeatedly to get the kind of visibility you need that will result in a spike in sales.

Most magazines and newspapers offer a discount on multiple ad insertions, which is known as selling "off the rate card." That means you're getting a discounted price that differs from the price on the publication's advertising rate card. But if you contract for just one or a few insertions, you can expect to pay full price.

Accessories entrepreneurs like California's Donna von Hoesslin who use print ads are very careful about where they advertise. For example, she advertises in publications that mirror her personal views about and commitment to environmentally friendly practices. If you don't have a hook like she does, another place to advertise that can be very cost-effective is your community's free newspaper. Of course, this only works if you have a brick-and-mortar or click-and-mortar retail store—if you're virtual or strictly wholesale, then local publications are of no value to you. However, if you're a wholesaler you might want to look into advertising in publications that cater to the retail fashion trade, including *Woman's Wear Daily* (wwd.com) or *Apparel News* (apparelnews.net).

Since you'll be selling high-end accessories, it's best to have your print ad professionally designed. You can easily find a freelance designer through your local Yellow Pages, professional advertising association, or university art department, as well as on the internet. Try Googling keywords like "commercial artist" or "graphic designer" and see who pops up.

When writing your ad, be sure to include an attention-getting headline, as well as pictures and details about your products (often, just a list of items will do), then provide full contact information, including your telephone number, website, and e-mail address. Your logo also should figure prominently in the ad. If writing isn't your forte, not to fear: You can find a freelance copywriter to handle the task. Often the designer you select can give you a referral to a copywriter with whom she has worked, or you can search for a writer the same way you prospected for a designer.

Yellow Pages

If you have a brick-and-mortar or click-and-brick store, you need to be in "the book," mostly because your competition is there already. When you have a business line installed in your store, you will automatically receive a line ad in the book, which is a one- or two-line listing that gives your store name, address, and phone number. Your local directory may also offer you the opportunity to include your website address, but you probably will have to pay a little extra for that benefit.

Depending on your promotional objectives, you may find that a line ad is sufficient. But if you're in a metro area with a lot of competition or in a resort area or other area that attracts a lot of vacationers, you might want to spend extra for a display ad. A display ad is a larger ad that's often boxed to set it off from other ads on the same page. The larger size gives you room to include more information

> **Tip...**
>
> **Smart Tip**
> Feel free to use the back of your business card for additional information that will be useful to your customers, such as store hours (if you have a brick-and-mortar business), a list of your product categories, a private ordering number, an image statement related to your business philosophy, or even testimonials ("Carried by Ms. Thang on the red carpet!").

about your store, including a list of merchandise, hours of operation, types of credit cards accepted, and so on. However, display ads can be somewhat pricey and may not give you enough return for the money. One good way to determine whether you might need a display ad is to look at your local phone directory and see how many of your competitors have display ads. If not many do, then you probably don't need one, either.

Also, in some markets you can place what's known as an expanded line ad, which gives you room for additional information without the higher cost of a standard display ad. One business owner we know of in the Southwest pays $60 a month for her 1-by-1-inch in-column ad and feels the money is well-spent.

Word-of-Mouth Advertising

If you maintain an inventory of stylish and up-to-date merchandise, are friendly and helpful when customers come through the door, and accept returns graciously and cheerfully, people will say positive things about you. Word-of-mouth (WOM) advertising is like money in the bank because it can result in sales to other people who heard good things about you. They, in turn, will talk to other people and . . . well, you get the idea.

But you don't have to stand by and hope people will talk about you over coffee or in the lingerie line at Nordstrom. Alexander Hiam, author of *Marketing for Dummies* (IDG Books), says it's possible to influence what your customers say about you. For example, doing something positive and visible in your community is an easy way to get people talking. Von Hoesslin, the California belt and jewelry designer, sponsors the local all-girl surf team (and supplies them with plenty of her jewelry to wear, by the way), gives away products for fundraising auctions, and so on.

"When people come in and ask me to sponsor something, I usually say 'yes,'" von Hoesslin says. "I give them overstock that isn't easy to move anyway. They're happy to get something nice for their event, and I clear out space for new things."

Another good way to influence WOM is by becoming involved in local business organizations, like the chamber of commerce or Rotary International. Attending "meet and greets," volunteering for committee work, or otherwise becoming involved in an organization's activities gives you instant visibility in the business community and helps you build a professional network. Then the next time a member of the organization needs a gift, he will remember that you're in the fashion accessories business and will probably stop in for a chat and a purchase. People like to do business with people they know and respect—so take advantage of that.

Promote Yourself

Finally, some of the best advertising you can muster up is self-generated and absolutely free—you simply wear or carry your own products. Adorn every outfit, from jeans to eveningwear, with something wonderful from your collection. (Don't forget to wear things you'd like to move at the end of the season or you're overstocked on—instant sales can result.) Change handbags as often as you change outfits so you give all the items in your product line equal time. Turn your scarves into your own personal signature item by learning how to tie them in as many ways as possible, then wear them with everything you own.

And don't think you're left out of the self-promotion loop if you're a man who sells women's accessories. Enlist your wife, significant other, and every other female in your life to act as walking billboards for your products. They'll love wearing all those new and pretty things—and you'll love the exposure you'll gain when people ask where they got them. Then, of course, tell them to whip out those business cards and distribute them freely, and you could easily find yourself on the way to new sales.

Sample Line Sheet with Pictures

Le Bel Sac LLC
www.lebelsac.com
877-887-8778
Spring '09 Collection

	Printemps Debussy Style #077-DB Full grain leather	$115
	Printemps Bleu Vista Style #077-BV Watered silk with patent trim	$100
	Printemps Tropic Soir Style #077-TS Pebbled leather	$125
	Printemps Bossa Nova Style #077-BN Full grain leather	$125
	Printemps Kiwi Satchel Style #077-KS Crocodile	$145

Minimum order: $500—Delivery: Minimum of 4–6 weeks
Terms: First order COD—Reorders: Net 15

Sample Line Sheet without Pictures

LIZASONIA
6127 La Salle Ave
Oakland, CA 94611
Owner:Liza Sonia Wallach
Ph: (001) 1-415-577-3684
Office: (001) 1-415-577-3684
Fax: (001) 1-415-441-4755
Email: Liza@LizaSonia.com
www.LizaSonia.com

Legend A
MC=Men's Cufflink
MR=Men's Ring
MB=Men's Bracelet
BMOP=Black Mother of Pearl Shell
PK=Packaging

*Last Update: 10/12/07 *** Prices subject to change until P.O. is accepted ****

LINE SHEET:Winter/Spring 2006

Category Name: Fine Silver (97% Thai Hill Tribe Silver) VPN #	Description	Weight/Length /Size	Wholesale Price # 1 (w/bag)	Wholesale Price #2 (Fancy Box)	Lead Time (weeks)/ In Stock (Quantity)	Minimum
LeafN	Fine Silver Necklalce	Can vary: 16-22 inches	$	$	in stock	3 pieces total any
						combo
LeafB	Fine Silver Bracelet	6.5 inches-8	$	$	in stock	
FlowerN	Fine Silver neckalce	Can vary: 16-22 inches	$	$	in stock	
FlowerB	Fine Silver Bracelet	6.5 inches-8	$	$	in stock	
SwirlN	Fine Silver Necklace	Can vary: 16-22 inches	$	$	in stock	
SwirlB	Fine Silver Bracelet	6.5 inches-8	$	$	in stock	

Category Name: Crystal, silk or silver collection *all can be made in any color VPN #	Description	Weight/Length/ Size	Wholesale Price # 1 (w/bag)	Wholesale Price #2 (Fancy Box)	Lead Time (weeks)/ In Stock (Quantity)	Minimum
Lariat short necklace	crystal/silk (any color)	about 24 inches	$	$	3 weeks/in stock	3 pieces
long lariat necklace	crystal/silk (any color)	60 inches	$	$	3 weeks/in stock	3 pieces

	VPN #	Description	Weight/Length/Size	Wholesale Price #1 (w/bag)	Wholesale Price #2 (Fancy Box)	Lead Time (weeks)/ In Stock (Quantity)	Minimum
necklace	small flower	crystal/silk (any color)	16-22 adjustable	$	$	3 weeks/in stock	3 pieces
necklace	little drops	crystal/silk (any color)	16-22 adjustable	$	$	3 weeks/in stock	3 pieces
earrings	crystEgrapes	grape cluster (any color)	1.5 inches long	$	$	3 weeks/in stock	5 pairs
earrings	crystEdropes	long drops	2.5 inches	$	$	3 weeks/in stock	5 pairs
earrings	crystEdrop	one large drop (small earrings)	1.25 inches	$	$	3 weeks/in stock	5 pairs
earrings	crystEdot	small drop	1 inch	$	$	3 weeks/in stock	5 pairs
earrings	crystEwater	large waterfall earrings; crystal and silver (any color)	3 inches	$	$	3 weeks/in stock	5 pairs
earrings	crystEBall	one ball	1.5 inches long	$	$	3 weeks/in stock	5 pairs

Category Name: Resin Rings (highest grade, sterling silver)	VPN #	Description	Weight/Length/Size	Wholesale Price #1 (w/bag)	Wholesale Price #2 (Fancy Box)	Lead Time (weeks)/ In Stock (Quantity)	Minimum
COLORS							
43- Light Blue	Dots	3 large dots: large ring	20 mm x 30 mm	$	$	2 months	
44-Violet	Hearts	3 hearts: med. size	27 mm x 12 mm	$	$	2 months	
46- Red	Logo Flower	3 logo flowers: large ring	20 mm x 30 mm	$	$	2 months	
TR905- White	Men's Square	Large Men's ring	25 mm x 15 mm	$	$	2 months	
31- Pink	Stars	Multi stars: large	20 mm x 30 mm	$	$	2 months	
34.43.28- yellow/blue/green	Band	Multi rectangles: logo	25 mm x 10 mm	$	$	2 months	
39- aqua green	Bubbles	Multi circles: med. size	27 mm x 12 mm	$	$	2 months	

Sample line sheet courtesy of Liza Sonia Wallach

Sales Order Form

YOUR LOGO
HERE

SALES ORDER

[Your Company Name]
[Your Company Slogan]

[Street Address], [City, ST ZIP Code]
Phone [000.000.0000] Fax [000.000.0000]
[e-mail]

TO [Name]
[Company Name]
[Street Address]
[City, ST ZIP Code]
[Phone]
Customer ID [ABC12345]

SHIP [Name]
TO [Company Name]
[Street Address]
[City, ST ZIP Code]
[Phone]
Customer ID [ABC12345]

SALESPERSON	JOB	SHIPPING METHOD	SHIPPING TERMS	DELIVERY DATE	PAYMENT TERMS	DUE DATE
					Due on receipt	

QTY	ITEM #	DESCRIPTION	UNIT PRICE	DISCOUNT	LINE TOTAL
				TOTAL DISCOUNT	
				SUBTOTAL	
				SALES TAX	
				TOTAL	

Make all checks payable to [Your Company Name]

Your Place
in Cyberspace

Back in Chapter 10, you read about the selling opportunities available to accessories business owners through the World Wide Web. In this chapter, you'll learn how to get your products out in cyberspace so fashionistas and other interested parties can get excited over them 24/7 and hopefully buy, buy, buy them all.

Getting Started

Your first step toward entering the cyber race for fashion accessory domination is to establish your own website. This is actually pretty easy to do these days. There are tons of easy-to-use software packages available to help you design your own website, and you may even find that your ISP gives you a certain amount of space on its server (often 1GB) for a personal website, along with a website-builder tutorial to help you create it.

However, we are not actually recommending that you take on the task yourself unless you have expertise in web development. After all, your business website has the potential to help you rake in the big bucks, so you'll want it to be both professionally designed and easily navigable. A lot goes into the making of a viable, navigable, and fun website, so you really should hire someone to do the job right, as California belt and jewelry designer Donna von Hoesslin did. "I do a lot of the web content myself, like the copy, plus I run the blog myself," she says. "But I have a webmaster who does the technical stuff, updates the site, gives it a new look and builds new pages when I need them."

You can find a web designer online, through the Yellow Pages and through professional organizations. As with other professionals, a word-of-mouth reference is usually the best way to get a lead to someone competent and creative.

Creating Content

But let's take a step back for a moment. Before you start looking for a web designer, it's important to consider exactly what you want your website to say. Toward that end, come up with a list of questions you think your customers would have when searching for the type of accessories you offer. For instance, here are examples of the kinds of questions buyers might have for a jewelry designer:

- What types of jewelry do you offer?
- Who designs the jewelry?
- Is it handmade?
- What kinds of gemstones do you use?
- Can you make a custom piece for me from my own sketch or idea?
- Who's wearing your jewelry (i.e., celebrities)?
- What is the price range of your jewelry?
- Where can I buy it?
- Can I buy it online? How do I place an order?
- How long will it take for my order to reach me?
- Should I insure the package?

And here are some typical questions for a handbag, belt, scarf, and/or hat business owner:

- What types of accessories do you offer?
- Who designs them?
- Are the accessories handmade?
- How long is the belt or scarf? What are the dimensions of the handbag or bag? What is the drop on the handles?
- What material is it made of?
- Do you use vegan leather?
- What color is the handbag, scarf, etc.?
- Who's wearing your accessories (i.e., celebrities)?
- What is the price range of your accessories?
- Where can I buy them?
- How do I place an order?
- How long will it take for my order to reach me?
- Should I insure the package?

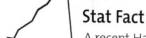

Stat Fact

A recent Harris Interactive poll indicated that 178 million adult Americans (79 percent) are now online. Of these users, 30 percent are college educated and 53 percent have household incomes above $50,000. The heaviest users are adults aged 18 to 39, who make up 45 percent of the cyber population—and are the biggest fashion consumers.

Once you've compiled your own list of questions, you have a good start on the content of your website, as well as content that can be featured on a frequently asked questions page. Basically, each question above represents a page on the site, although some of the information, such as shipping information, can be grouped together as part of a single page.

If you consider yourself fairly creative or you have writing experience, you might want to write the web copy yourself. However, you should know there is a knack to writing great web copy. As with other types of advertising copy, it should focus on reader benefits, and be rich in keywords, which are the words embedded in the text that will give your website a high search engine ranking. Keywords actually appear throughout your website, as well as in title tags, which are small pieces of HTML code that appear in the top bar of your browser. These title tags are what cause your website to appear as an entry on a search engine browser. For example, if you are selling handcrafted shell beach jewelry, your title tag might be "handcrafted shell beach jewelry." That way, the search engine will find your website when a person types these words or any combination of them (i.e., shell jewelry, handcrafted beach jewelry, etc.). You'll find more information about keywords later in this chapter.

If all this is making your head spin or you just don't have the knack for copywriting, then you should seriously consider hiring a copywriter with web page experience

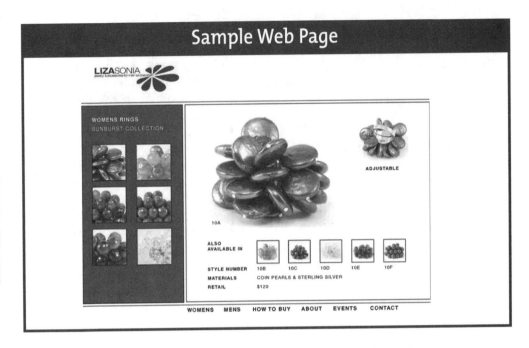

Sample Web Page

to write your website copy. (Make sure you turn over that list of questions you formulated as a starting point.) Then, of course, you'll need a web designer to take that copy and turn it into HTML language, another thing we recommend farming out to an experienced professional. It may cost you up to $2,000 to get a website up and running, but considering how important an internet presence is for both new and experienced business owners, it's money well spent.

One thing you should discuss in great detail with your web designer is the look of your site. If you'll be selling upscale accessories, you'll want your website to mirror that upscale look. You can do that by keeping the page design clean and uncluttered (which keeps the emphasis on your beautiful accessories) and the copy lively yet succinct. In addition, it's not necessary to have lengthy descriptions—when it comes to jewelry and other accessories, a picture truly is worth a thousand words, plus readers really prefer *not* to have to scroll down as they read. Try to have the pages formatted so all the information can appear in a single screen shot in order to make them as user-friendly as possible. See above for an example of a well-designed accessories web page.

Organizing the Site

Among the basic elements you should include on your fashion accessories website are:

- *Welcome page.* A brief introduction describing the range of accessories you offer will entice visitors to delve deeper into the website. It also should have a navigation bar at or near the top of the page where visitors click to go to other pages within the site. The navigation bar can include any of the elements discussed below, as well as links to other information on the site, and any news or information that might be of interest to readers.

- *Collections.* List the products you offer, organized by product type and with photographs or drawings. For example, Brooke Sobel, the San Francisco handbag designer, organizes her products into two categories: Italian Collection and the intriguingly named Modern Vintage Collection. Clicking on either of those links transports the visitor electronically to pictures of the featured handbags.

- *Price list.* If you sell wholesale, you might want to include prices on a dedicated password-protected page so only wholesale customers can see them. Never publish your wholesale prices where the general public can see them.

- *Your credentials/experience.* This information can be placed under an "About" or "Bio" link, and should discuss both your background and the reasons why you're qualified to create and/or sell the fabulous fashions you offer. While it can be a plus to mention your educational background, especially if you've studied fashion design, what's more important to readers is the personal experience that makes you a trusted fashion accessories source. For instance, Donna von Hoesslin, the California belt and jewelry designer, is an experienced surfer who sells ethically manufactured surf items. This is personal expertise that is important to surfers (ocean surfers, that is) because the surfer community is so close-knit.

- *Photo gallery.* Include lots of photos of models carrying or wearing your accessories, both to show how great they look with the latest fashion, as well as to give customers an idea how to use them, if appropriate. If you're selling scarves, for example, you might show different ways to tie scarves, or even offer a primer of scarf-tying techniques with step-by-step instructions so customers are not afraid they won't be able to reproduce the fashionable tying

> ### Smart Tip
> Flash animation is creative and fun, but it's not always appropriate for a business website. In addition, if it takes too long to play, visitors can get annoyed and move on to the next flash-less website. If you really want to use flash, make sure there's a "skip intro" link on the page so visitors can bypass it quickly.

> ### Bright Idea
> In this age of spam and identity theft, it's important to include a privacy statement in plain English on your website that stresses that you'll never sell visitors' names to third parties. This signals to potential clients that you respect their privacy and may make them more willing to shop your site.

Sample Model Release

MODEL RELEASE

By signing this form I give unrestricted permission to _____
to use, display, publish, and otherwise distribute photographs of me (or photos in which I appear) that are in print, digital, or other forms.

I release _____ from any and all claims arising from such use.

This agreement is governed by the laws of the state of _____ and represents the entire agreement.

_____
Printed name

_____
Address

_____
Signature   Date

technique you've illustrated. In addition, if you're lucky enough to get photos of celebrities sporting your accessories (ether because they bought an item or you sent them a sample), you can include those photos here. However, check first to find out if your state has a regulation called "right of publicity" (most do). This protects the ways in which photos of public figures can be used. For more information about the right of publicity, check out the article at pub law.com/rightpriv.html.

Obtaining a signed photo release is often enough to get the right to use a photo, as well as give you some protection against lawsuits. (Some, because somewhere, somehow, someone will still find a way to sue.) You'll see a simple model release you can use above, although you might want to run it by your attorney to make sure it's adequate for your purposes, just in case.

Incidentally, you are less liable to stir up legal trouble if you simply name the person who was spotted using your accessories rather than showing your product *in situ*. Speak to your attorney to find out whether it's safe to name-drop on your website.

- *Stores*. If you're selling through retail stores other than your own, you might wish to include a list of the stores that stock your accessories. Often, a list of names is enough, although if the store sells merchandise online, you might provide a hyperlink to the store as a way to spur visitors to buy.

- *Press clippings.* Publicity is very important to any new business, which is why you'll find a discussion of publicity techniques in Chapter 15. Once those publicity efforts start working, you'll want to share them with customers. You either can excerpt positive comments in the media that spotlight you and your company, reproduce the magazine or newspaper page where the article appears, or provide a hyperlink so readers can click on it and be transported to the website where it appears. A press section also provides valuable information to other reporters who may be interested enough to write about your accessories in their publication.

- *Resources.* Providing a list of resources that might be useful to your customers is a way to build customer goodwill and possibly inspire them to make additional purchases. The scarf-tying tutorial mentioned earlier is the type of resource that customers find useful. Others that might be used on a jewelry website include: a list of gemstones, a list of birthstones by month, a discussion about the color and cut of gemstones, and jewelry care information. In addition, washing and care instructions for other accessories, like scarves and handbags, are good to include.

- *Contact information.* Here's where you include your business address, phone and fax numbers, and e-mail and web address. Keep in mind, however, if you're homebased it's neither necessary nor recommended that you publish your home address. To make it easier for customers to find you, include a link to a mapping site like Mapquest.com or maps.google.com so prospective customers can easily obtain driving directions to your store. This is also a good place to include your business hours.

- *Other links.* As mentioned earlier, you should compile a frequently asked questions list that might cover issues like shipping, ethical/sustainable practices, payment information, and anything else that you think customers might like to know that doesn't fit into the categories mentioned above.

Blog On

The internet has spawned a lot of unique opportunities for entrepreneurs. But the online tool that may have the most potential for ramping up your sales and increasing your visibility in the world of fashion accessories is the weblog, or blog for short.

A blog is an online journal that reflects the opinions and thoughts of the author. Blogs are arranged in reverse chronological order just as an e-mail has the most recent post at the top every time it's exchanged between two people. Typically, a blog contains a main post section, photos, a readers' comments section, and links to other blogs or websites. Some blogs even have advertising, which could happen if your blog catches on.

While many blogs are written just for fun, others are viewed as real workhorses. Entrepreneurs and even large companies increasingly are using blogs as marketing tools, both as a way to increase their visibility on search engines and to build long-lasting relationships with their customers.

Launching a blog is easy. Just sign up with one of the many blog-hosting services online. There are quite a few freebies, but they're not always particularly easy to use and they probably offer limited, if any, customer support. So a better choice might be a service like TypePad, which offers 1GB storage, professionally designed templates, professional service and support, and much more, for $14.95 a month. But as with everything in the cyber world, prices are competitive, so shop around.

In the meantime, check out Sparkle Plenty, New York jewelry entrepreneur Ruta Fox's blog, at divinediamonds.com. Also, the blog at fashion-incubator.com contains a lot of cut and sew information that is very useful for anyone who will be making soft goods like handbags or scarves.

Naming Rights

Firming up your web content is just the first step to getting your website online. The next thing you must do is select a domain name, which is a name that uniquely identifies your website. Obviously, the best domain name is one that mirrors your company name. However, your domain name must be unique in cyberspace, and it's possible that the name is already in use. For example, let's say your name is Beth Taylor and you create handcrafted jewelry. A clever company name would be Taylor Made Jewelry. But a Google search indicates that taylormadejewelry.com is already in use, so you'd have to pick another name, like, say, taylormadejewelrybybeth.com (but of course, an address that's too long can be a liability).

It's easy to verify that your domain name is unique. You simply pick a company that provides domain names and do a search on its website. If it is unique, you pony up a few bucks to reserve it, and you can use it forever as long as you continue to renew it. And we do mean just a few bucks—a domain provider like GoDaddy.com charges a mere $9.99 or less per year for a new domain name registration, while Domain.com, one of the original domain name companies, charges $8.75 a year, plus assorted additional fees. (When it first debuted, Domain.com was charging $70 a year!) Another domain registrar we know of, namesecure.com,

offers one-year domains for $8.95 or less, depending on how long you sign up for, and even offers domains for $3.99 a year if you also sign up for web hosting (discussed below). Since there are so many domain providers these days, you might want to ask your web designer or computer consultant for a recommendation.

Hosting Your Cyberspace

The next step in the web page process is selecting a web host, which is a cyber business that shares its server with clients like you so your website can be accessible 24/7. As with domain companies, there are tons of web hosts, including Yahoo Hosting, EarthLink Web Hosting, and HostMonster. In addition, most domain name providers like GoDaddy.com also offer web hosting, which is convenient because you can get both services in the same place. There even are free web hosts, but they often have size limitations, insist that you put banner advertising on your site, and require you to use their online tools to build your site. They're also notorious for excessive downtime, which can kill your cyber business if it happens too often. Since web hosting is so inexpensive—around $4.95 a month or less—and because it's a business expense anyway, it's usually better to sign up with one of the larger or better known web hosts.

▲

Keywords

You'll remember that earlier we mentioned that search engine keywords are the key—pardon the pun—to getting customers to find you in cyberspace. When searching for scarves, for example, they might type in "silk scarf 30 inch," and if these words appear on your site, it would pop up in the search results. Von Hoesslin uses a wide variety of keywords, including "shell belts," "surf jewelry" and "beaded belts," so anyone cruising the web for surfer-related products would find her easily.

> ### Bright Idea
>
> Register your website on as many search engines as possible to increase the chances that fashionistas will find it. Try using a service like Add Me (addme.com), which will submit your domain to the top 20 search engines for free. Want to be on hundreds of search engines? That costs $99 for a one-year subscription.

As you can see, the trick is to select words that are very specific to your products, without being so narrow or specialized that surfers won't think of them when mulling over which keywords to search. At the same time, they can't be so general that they result in too many hits, which is unhelpful because then you'll rank low on the results list. Research shows that most people don't look beyond a page or two of search results, so you want to make sure your site is among the first ones that show up.

Here's a list of core keywords that might be appropriate for various fashion accessories businesses:

- Designer, upscale, luxury, high end, high quality, handcrafted, custom, fashion
- Accessory
- Handbag, leather handbag, bag, leather bag
- Purse, leather purse
- Organizer bag, minibag
- Earrings, hoops, necklace, lariat, bracelet
- Gemstone, beaded, gold, sterling silver, hammered (as in gold), pearl, freshwater pearl
- Scarf, head scarf, hand-rolled edge, silk, floral
- Hat, cap, feather, hatband
- Belt, buckle, leather belt, calfskin belt
- Wholesale anything (wholesale scarf, wholesale belt, etc.)

Pay-Per-Click

Keywords are great for attracting attention, but if you've ever typed search terms into a browser and been bombarded with 220,000 or more hits, then you know that keywords aren't always enough to attract the kind of attention you want. So you might want to try pay-per-click (PPC) advertising. PPC advertising links appear in a specific section of search engine pages, often down the right side of the screen, when someone types keywords into a browser. When someone clicks on one of these links, he or she is taken directly to the advertiser's website, and the advertiser pays for that hit.

PPC advertising can be a valuable marketing tool because it's a way to attract the attention of a person who presumably wants to buy something at that very moment. The good news is the cost of PPC advertising can be as low as one-tenth of a cent to 50 cents per click, which is billed monthly and payable by credit card. The bad news is, the conversion rate of "click to order" from PPCs is very low—about 1.5 percent.

Although Google is the best-known search engine, it's not the only company that offers PPCs. (Search on pay-per-click to find other companies you can check out.) But you don't automatically get PPCs just by handing over your credit card number; you actually bid on them, and it's not hard to rack up thousands of dollars in PPC costs every month. For this reason, you might want to start out using keywords and progress to PPC advertising after your business has a chance to grow and prosper.

Virtual Shopping

The product descriptions are written and your website is operational. Now it's time to make some money. To do that, you need two more electronic tools: a virtual shopping cart and a merchant account.

Powered by specialized software that's integrated into your website, a virtual shopping cart allows customers to "select" merchandise by clicking on an "Add to Cart" button. This deposits the merchandise into an electronic holding area, where it remains until the customer clicks on the "Checkout" button. After providing billing/shipping information, the customer is directed to a payment page, where credit card information is entered. This information is usually protected by Secure Sockets Layer (SSL) encryption, which makes it impossible for hackers to steal the customer's personal information.

That's the process. To make it happen, you need electronic commerce (aka shopping cart) software. One reputable product to check out is ShopSite (shopsite.com), which allows you to create an online store from scratch (if you don't have a website already), or add a shopping cart to existing web pages. The monthly cost to use ShopSite is $9 to $39, plus the cost of web hosting. You also might want to check into MerchandiZer (merchandizer.com) and Network Solutions (ecommerce.network solutions.com), or you can Google "shopping cart software" to find many other products to select from. Need help deciding? Talk to your web developer.

Gateway to Sales

Basically a middleman between an online shopping cart and the financial networks that process online payment transactions, a payment gateway is an important e-commerce tool because it allows e-businesses and brick-and-click businesses to accept credit card and e-check payments securely. But here's the catch: Gateways have a breathtaking list of fees, which typically include a setup fee (around $200), monthly maintenance fee ($30), per-transaction fee (55 cents each), Visa/Mastercard inquiry fee (24 cents each), mail order telephone order fee (MOTO) for card-not-present transactions (2.28 percent), swipe fee (1.75 percent), and credit card statement fee ($5). Kind of makes you wonder how much you're left with at the end of all the processing.

You can select your own gateway, or you can pick an electronic commerce software (like ShopSite) that has its own preferred provider lists for both the merchant and payment gateway accounts. If you do want to pick the provider, check out Authorize.net (authorize.net), PaySimple (paysimple.com) or PayFlo Pro (a product of PayPal; go to paypal.com, then click on Products & Services). But shop around. Gateway rates definitely are competitive and are falling as more providers enter the market.

The final step in the online shopping cart process is to verify that your customer's credit is good or that there is sufficient cash in his/her account to cover the charge or debit purchase. For this you need a merchant account, which is an electronic clearinghouse that confirms that it's safe to accept the credit or debit card as payment. The process is simple. Once the electronic commerce software tallies everything up and adds the appropriate state taxes and/or shipping charges, the total is transmitted to a payment gateway. The processing is handled by the merchant account, which then sends information back to the gateway indicating whether the transaction has been approved or declined. If approved, the order is confirmed and the funds are transferred to the merchant account so they can be scheduled for transfer into the seller's bank account. All of this happens in a matter of seconds, which frees your merchant account up to process the next transaction. Naturally, there are fees associated with both processes. See Chapter 16 for more information.

The Power
of the Press

Baby doll tops in retro prints. Animal print belts and bags. Capris and cropped pants. They're all recent fashion trends that came to life on a designer's drawing board, debuted on designer runways, then became *the* look for the young and fashionable before spreading to the ladies who lunch, soccer moms, and every other woman who wants to look young and hip.

This is a diverse buyer's market, to be sure, but generally speaking, those buyers find out about what's new and exciting in the same ways—they check out what the Beautiful People are wearing on the red carpet at Hollywood award shows and on the daytime soaps, they read fashion magazines, and they prowl around the mall. Your job as a small-business owner is to make sure those fashion movers and shakers know about your fashion accessories, too, and the way to do that is to launch your own personal publicity campaign.

As you know from Chapter 13, there are a lot of solid ways to advertise your fashion accessories, most of which will cost you. So you'll probably be delighted to know that positive press usually doesn't cost much aside from the cost of your time to prepare succinct and carefully targeted publicity materials, and perhaps the cost of an accessory or two sent to influential people. In this chapter, you'll learn about the various publicity and public relations tools that are particularly beneficial for fashion accessories businesses—and budgets.

News Releases

The media is always hungry for news about up-and-coming fashion designers and their product lines, as well as any other fashion product brought to market, and the easiest way to get press coverage for *yours* is by sending out news releases. Also known as press releases, these little publicity gems are your most powerful publicity tools. They're usually one to two pages long and provide details—preferably in sparkling and evocative language—about your fabulous fashion items. The idea is to pique the interest of influential fashionistas—i.e., editors and writers—at national and regional magazines, newspapers, and even fashion websites and blogs in the hope that they'll devote some space to your products in their print or virtual publication.

Naturally, this kind of exposure is golden—and the price is right. However, there's a catch. There's no guarantee that your news release will actually be published because editors often treat them either as idea starters or as "filler" material; that is, if there's a hole to be filled on a page, information from a news release can be dropped in. That's why you'll find that out of the 500 or so carefully crafted words you write, only 100 or fewer will actually appear in print. But trust us—even a news brief can be enough to start an avalanche of new accessories orders cascading your way. So don't be offended if your painstakingly crafted release gets carved up. It's still valuable free publicity no matter the length.

Some fashion accessories stories that might be of interest to an editor include:

- The opening of your new brick-and-mortar location
- Establishment of a new website
- Details about new product lines

- Trunk shows showcasing the season's new accessories
- Holiday gift ideas
- Charitable contributions (e.g., for a hospital's fund-raising silent auction) or green activities (giving something back to the planet, like California belt and jewelry designer Donna von Hoesslin does)

While all these are viable story ideas, it's important to note that they should be breaking news, not manufactured news sent just for the sake of sending something, and they must be targeted toward the appropriate audience. For example, the editor of *Women's Wear Daily* is probably not going to be interested in a story about how you used Six Sigma principles to set up your manufacturing process, while "What Not to Wear" can't use a release on your fabulous new location. The best thing to do is to read issues of the publication (or watch the show) to which you wish to submit, paying attention to:

Beware!

Make sure you have enough product on hand or can ramp up production quickly before sending out new releases about your merchandise. If you're lucky enough to get good exposure in a fashion publication, you could find yourself inundated with orders, and if you can't fulfill those orders quickly, your accessories career could be over before it begins.

- *Focus.* Publications generally have a very specialized audience, so if you're designing or selling expensive handbags, for example, a young teen-focused publication is probably not the place to pitch your bags. Likewise, you wouldn't submit news about your whimsical puppy and kitty sterling silver jewelry collection to *Vogue*. (But it might be right for *Glamour*, which has a younger and more fun vibe—but you'll never know unless you read the publication.)

- *Columns.* Fashion magazines often have a variety of "departments" focusing on different aspects of the fashion industry. Get acquainted with those columns and send your releases directly to their editors rather than to the magazine's managing editor. You'll have a better chance of getting a reading that way.

- *Editorial schedule.* Publications compile an annual schedule of topics to be covered that is available for anyone to view (often right on the website). Review the editorial schedule of the publications you're interested in to see whether they have planned issues that mesh nicely with your particular product or collection, then time the delivery of your release to coincide with the deadline date provided by the publication.

- *Publication schedule.* Magazines have a long lead time—often four to six months—so releases about seasonal merchandise must be timed to arrive just as far ahead. You'll find the pertinent deadlines on each magazine's editorial schedule.

▲

Also, just because you're designing or selling fashion accessories doesn't mean fashion magazines are the only places suitable to receive your news releases. Instead, think outside the box and consider any publication that might be a good conduit for your publicity efforts. For example, von Hoesslin sells surfer-designed and inspired products, so surfer and travel publications are a natural place to submit news releases about her collection.

Bright Idea

Although print and virtual publications are the most likely audiences for news releases, cable TV fashion shows like *What Not to Wear* should be on your news release list, too. Just imagine one day seeing your accessories on the air in the French-manicured hands of a cable TV host like Stacy London of *What Not to Wear*.

Also, just because you're designing or selling fashion accessories doesn't mean fashion magazines are the only places suitable to receive your news releases. Instead, think outside the box and consider any publication that might be a good conduit for your publicity efforts. For example, von Hoesslin sells surfer-designed and inspired products, so surfer and travel publications are a natural place to submit news releases about her collection.

Writing the Release

If you can write a logically developed, reader-oriented letter, then you should be able to write a news release. See page 169 for a sample. But if you bypassed a career in writing or public relations for a very good reason (e.g., you can't write your way out of a paper bag), you might want to hire a freelance writer. Freelance writers will usually charge by the hour or the project, and you can expect to pay about $100 to $250 for someone to develop a one-page release. You can find freelance writers by placing an ad on Craigslist.org, through professional advertising organizations, Elance.com, your local chamber of commerce, and university journalism advertising departments. You could also use a public relations firm, but they tend to be pretty expensive for a startup business owner.

Sending the Release

Once you've finalized your copy, you're ready to send out your news release. It's really important to send the release to a specific person rather than to the "Editor," so you'll want to compile contact information for the right person at each publication. This information can generally be found on the publication's website, but you may have to call to get the right name and contact information.

These days, most editors prefer to receive information by e-mail or fax rather than by snail mail. Use the words "News release" followed by the headline of the release in the subject line (for example: "News release—New collection of silk scarves reduces carbon footprint").

Smart Tip

If you need to delay publication of your news release for a particular reason (like until the magazine with a feature on your new fall collection hits the newsstands), substitute the words "Release date: Embargo until (date)" for the "For Immediate Release" line.

Sample News Release

FOR IMMEDIATE RELEASE

Date: June 4, 20xx

Media contact: Suzanne Phair

Telephone: (520) 555-5923

Exclusive "green" jewelry line debuts at AccessoriesTheShow

SEDONA, ARIZONA—Brilliant crystals and iridescent shells. Shimmering recycled glass beads and lustrous pearls. When such reclaimed items from nature's bounty are woven, inset, and hand-tied into high-style, earth-friendly jewelry, something magical happens—something that can take your sales to new heights for the coming holiday season.

The magic starts with the "Phair Enough" line of environmentally friendly necklaces, bracelets, and earrings from Phyllis Phasions. Imagined by green jewelry designer Phyllis Phair, this line of exquisitely wrought jewelry will debut exclusively at AccessoriesTheShow, slated for Javitz Center in Manhattan on Aug. 2-4, 200x.

You can also experience the magic for yourself during a private showing of the line on Aug. 1 at the Gem Hotel, just steps away from Javitz Center. A limited number of appointments are available for retail buyers. To request a private appointment, call (520) 555-5923.

# # #

When e-mailing, send the release as an attachment, and as a courtesy, paste it into the body of the e-mail as well, just in case the recipient prefers not to open attachments.

If you must use snail mail, send the release to the appropriate editor in a No. 10 envelope—preferably one that's professionally printed with your company name and return address in the upper left corner. You also can type "News release—dated material" on the outside of the envelope if you wish.

Finally, be sure to include a copy of your most recent line sheet with *retail* (never wholesale) prices, which the editor will need when he/she writes or edits your material.

Calling All Editors

To increase the chances that your release will be used—or read, for that matter—contact the editor about a week after you send the release and politely inquire about whether the release was received and if it's likely to appear in print. If not, ask what types of information the editor is looking for so you'll know how to craft future releases. Time releases to arrive midweek to increase the likelihood that they'll be read.

Press Kits

Another way to spread the word about your company is by creating a simple press kit. Its primary purpose is to give anyone interested in your company—usually reporters, investors, and other analysts—background and vital statistics about the company. Toward that end, your press kit should include:

- *Backgrounder.* A one-page document giving general information about the company (when it was founded, by whom, and for what purpose).
- *Bio.* A few paragraphs about yourself, including information about your previous business experience and education.
- *Photo.* A professional 5-by-7-inch black-and-white photo of yourself is best. If you have a signature product (like Ruta Fox's Ah Ring, for instance), include a photo of that as well.
- *Line sheet.* A product sheet listing the retail prices of your current collection (again, never the wholesale prices).
- *News releases.* Copies of your most recent releases.
- *Clips.* Recent clippings from newspapers and magazines that show your company and/or products in a positive light.
- *Contact information.* A sheet with your brick-and-mortar address (for a retail store) or mailing address (for a homebased business), as well as phone, cell phone and fax numbers, and website and e-mail addresses.

Since you won't need a ton of press kits on hand when you start your business, you can build them yourself as you need them. It's customary to organize the materials in a pocket folder, which is perfectly sized to send out in a 9-by-12-inch envelope. While you can have your pocket folders custom printed for a really snazzy and professional look (about $500 for 100 folders with slits for business cards), a standard pocket folder from your local office supply store works fine. If you go the do-it-yourself route, however, you should print stickers with your logo and company name and affix them to the front of the folder so recipients can see at a glance whom the press kit is from.

> **Smart Tip** *Tip...*
>
> Be sure to send a line sheet along when you send out press kits, news releases or other materials to the media. However, make sure you develop a line sheet with retail rather than wholesale prices for this purpose. Never divulge your wholesale prices to anyone other than a prospective retail buyer.

Your press kit should always be accompanied by a brief letter introducing yourself and your company and telling why your company and products are newsworthy. In addition, you should prepare a downloadable version of the press kit for your website. This is both more convenient for reporters and others who might want information on demand, as well as more cost-effective for you because you won't have to spend a lot of money printing out and mailing materials.

Brooke Sobel, the San Francisco handbag designer, actually recommends having a downloadable version of your press kit instead of paper. "Editors just throw it away after they've looked at it," she says. "So make it basic and e-mail it whenever possible."

You also can make it creative to catch the attention of editors, as von Hoesslin does. Her press kit is printed on a single sheet of recycled paper—literally—and is folded origami-style into a little packet about 3 by 5.5 inches. When people request samples, she sends this "kit" with a pair of earrings tucked inside. If they want additional information, like a line sheet, she refers them to a special "retailers"-only website that shows her wholesale prices, which also serves as her product catalog since this environmentally conscious wholesaler doesn't have a paper catalog.

> **Bright Idea**
>
> Magazine editors love to feature new designers, so take advantage of their interest and send a press kit, news release, product photos, and other materials right before the debut of your first collection or product line. You only get one shot at this kind of "first," so max out the opportunities.

Related to the press kit is a press book, which is a binder or other type of book in which you have placed copies of magazines and/or articles in which your products are featured or mentioned. The idea is to show buyers that your product has come to the attention of the public because that makes it an easier sell, so you'll want to take your press book with you to appointments with buyers or when you're exhibiting at trade shows.

Product Placement

If you've ever watched Oprah Winfrey bestow each member of her studio audience with a product related to the day's program content (like when Tom Cruise guested and each audience member received a boxed set of all his films), then you know the power of samples. You can do the same type of thing, albeit on a smaller scale, to catch the attention of influential media types. If you're launching a new collection, for instance, you might want to send your signature item to a list of carefully selected editors. It's a great way to get maximum exposure for your accessories, although even at wholesale prices, it can be a pricey proposition. Your best bet is to dole out the samples sparingly and only to those who are truly influential or who work at the most influential publications.

Another person to get to know is the fashion stylist(s) who works on the fashion publications you're most interested in infiltrating. A fashion stylist is the person responsible for rounding up the clothing, shoes, and other accessories needed for a photo shoot. By sending photos and line sheets of the products in your collection to stylists on a regular basis, you up your chances of having one or more of your accessories featured in a future issue of the magazine.

If a product strikes a chord with a stylist because he or she is planning a particular photo shoot, you may be asked to lend one or more samples for the shoot. Always have an agreement in writing about where the product(s) will be used and when you can expect it to be returned. You also should have a clause that says that you'll expect payment for merchandise that's not returned by the designated due date. Just make sure to give the stylist a reasonable return deadline since photo shoots are often done on location and it may take a while for your samples to be shipped back to you.

You usually can find the names of fashion stylists in the masthead of your chosen publication. In addition, a directory known as *Le Book* (lebook.com) lists stylists (search on "Style" under "Multi-criteria search").

Another way to make samples work for you is to get them on the arm, around the neck, or in the hands of a celebrity. However, as Brooke Sobel points out, "Christie Brinkley has one of my bags, but without a photograph, it's not worth anything."

You can, however, mention on your website or in your promotional materials that your fashion accessories are favorites of the Beautiful People. For example, Sobel says on her website, "Today, Brooke's dazzling jewelry and funky handbags grace the bodies of A-list celebrities like Julia Roberts and Eva Longoria."

The best way to reach celebrities is through their stylist or publicist. You often can find the names of these folks on the internet.

Wholesale Tradeshows

> **Bright Idea**
>
> Be sure to collect a business card from every visitor to your trade show booth so you can follow up with that person after the show is over. Be sure to jot a few notes on the back of the card so you'll remember details like which products you discussed, quantities, colors, and any other useful information.

If you're planning to sell to retailers, you might want to consider participating in a wholesale trade show. These shows attract thousands of buyers, which gives you invaluable exposure that's especially important for a new fashion accessories business owner. The fashion industry's largest and longest running accessories trade show is AccessoriesTheShow, which is held in New York in January, May, and August during market weeks, as well as annually in Las Vegas. The show features 30 product categories and more than 900 collections, all of which are upscale and designer brands, so this trade show isn't for every new accessories business owner.

Another well-established and very large trade show held in Las Vegas is MAGIC, which offers clothing and footwear in addition to fashion accessories. It attracts 120,000 buyers from 80 countries, and more than 4,000 companies, 5,000 brands, and 20,000 product lines are featured at the show. Contact information for both these show is also in the Appendix.

There are also a number of smaller regional trade shows, including an important show in Chicago, that you may wish to consider. You can find a list of the larger accessories trade shows at apparelsearch.com/trade_show_by_category_accessories.htm.

The benefits of exhibiting at a trade show are obvious—you'll get a chance to speak to a lot of prospective buyers and hopefully will walk away with some orders. But it can be pricey. For instance, it costs $3,995 just to exhibit at the MAGIC show, which doesn't include the cost of the hardwall or softwall booth that goes into the space, plus there's no guarantee you'll get even a single order. Still, when you're just starting out, you need the exposure, so it's something to consider.

Trade Show Booths for Fun and Profit

Large trade shows like MAGIC will happily rent an exhibit booth to you—at great cost. But if you're planning to do a lot of trade shows, you may wish to purchase your own. Amazingly, softwall booths, which stand up to 10 feet high on a framework rather like an umbrella that simply pops open, can be broken down and stuffed into storage containers that are actually light enough to transport yourself (albeit with a hand dolly). They're also very easy to assemble. They start at around $2,000, including fabric drapes, lights, and graphics.

Hardwall booths, on the other hand, usually stand 8 feet tall and have laminate or plywood panels that are covered with fabric. Obviously they're heavier and more difficult to assemble. They start at about $2,500.

A third type of display is the tabletop, which is exactly as the name implies. This type of "booth" is much more affordable at $500 and up. But be sure to contact the exhibition company before you buy any of these booths. Some shows, including MAGIC, have very strict requirements on what's acceptable on the trade show floor.

Networking

Unless you live in New York or Los Angeles, which are hotbeds of fashion design, you might not appreciate the value of networking. After all, networking is meant to generate new opportunities that can lead to sales, and if you're designing hats in Podunk, Iowa, you might find it hard to believe that you could possibly interact with anyone who could send business your way.

However, nothing could be farther from the truth. Every person you meet is a potential retail buyer. For that matter, every person you meet could even lead you to wholesale business or important business opportunities. Case in point: New York jewelry entrepreneur Ruta Fox, the creator of the Ah Ring, found a valued business contact through Match.com, of all places.

"I have no life beyond making money hand over fist," she says with a laugh. "The only men I ever see are the FedEx and UPS guys, so I decided to try Match.com. The first guy I had dinner with was in the jewelry business, and when I told him about the problems I was having getting rings from overseas fast enough to fill orders, he told me he could hook me up with a local diamond wholesaler and a factory, and I'd be able to pick up the rings in Manhattan in two weeks."

Fox knew providence at work when she saw it. "This man was guided to me to help me over a huge obstacle," she says emphatically. "The rings are consistently of amazing quality, and they are available at the price my psychic predicted!"

You might not meet the manufacturer of your dreams the way Fox did (and by the way, the personal relationship didn't work out), but you definitely will meet people who might turn out to be valuable business contacts. So get involved with your local chamber of commerce or an economic development organization, both of which will offer valuable networking resources to their members. The cost to join such organizations is usually nominal, and the benefits are enormous, both in terms of exposure for your business and the opportunity to exchange ideas and barter services with the owners of other businesses.

Working the Crowd

As a business owner, you should always be looking for opportunities to befriend or become acquainted with people who provide services or products that are even loosely related to things fashionable and stylish, since everyone is a potential source of leads. Take the owner of a dry-cleaning store, for instance. He could have a customer who's looking for a fabulous belt to replace one that was lost (although hopefully not by the dry cleaner). The local hair salon owner might have a Red Hat Society member/customer who is a passionate collector of dramatic hats to wear to chapter meetings. The bridal salon owner who admires your necklace at a city council meeting might be thinking about adding a new line of wedding jewelry to her store. And so it goes. Of course, when you make those connections, be sure to return the favor and refer business back to them. Such reciprocal relationships benefit everyone and cement your position as a valued member of the local business community.

Finances
for Fashionistas

Fashion might be all about flash and dash, but something more fundamental is required to keep the show running—and that something is cash; a whole lot of it, in some cases. So in this chapter, you'll see a rundown of what kind of scratch it takes to keep a small business like yours humming along every month, as well as some projections on how you'll offset those liabilities so you can make a living in the fabulous world of fashion accessories.

Income and Operating Expenses

In Chapter 7, you read about how important it was to have a good bookkeeper or accountant on your team, both to keep your finances in good order and to free you up from the more mundane aspects of the business that can crimp your creativity. That advice still holds, but at the same time, you still must have a good handle on what's happening with your business at all times. An easy way to do that is to create a simple monthly income/expenses (I&E) statement using the I&E worksheet on page 182. An I&E helps you estimate your operating costs and project your earnings, giving you an idea of where the business stands.

Don't despair if your math skills are fairly rudimentary. QuickBooks has easy I&E tracking that requires nothing more than plugging in figures to create usable worksheets. To get an idea of what's involved, look at the three sample I&Es starting on page 179 that show the expenses of three hypothetical fashion accessories businesses. Phyllis Phashions, a jewelry design/retail operation, is homebased and, as a result, has very low expenses. The midrange business, Fashion Faire, is strictly a reseller of scarves and belts—its owner purchases fashion accessories from manufacturers and resells them in a virtual store. The high-end business, Pamplemousse, is a handbag design company that manufactures its bags abroad. It also has a part-time helper.

Not all the expenses discussed in this chapter will apply to your business, but it's helpful to look at the full gamut of possibilities to get a good idea of what you might encounter along the way.

Read on for a rundown of the typical expenses you can expect to incur in your fashion accessories business.

Mortgage/Rent

If you're homebased, you won't have to worry about this very costly monthly expense, and in fact, it's usually a good idea to put off the big step of acquiring a retail store as long as possible. But we can't blame you if you want to take your accessories business public, especially if you happen to be setting up shop in a geographic area with a reliable stream of tourists or other potential customers. To give you an idea of the impact of leasing costs on your bottom line, we've included a rent figure on the high-end business's sample I&E that reflects the typical cost in a midsize market. Just be aware if you do decide to try a brick-and-mortar location that you'll have to sell a lot of earrings, bags, or belts just to pay the rent and utilities—which might not leave much to buy or manufacture new merchandise, the lifeblood of your business.

Sample Income & Expenses (Low End)

Phyllis Phashions

Projected Monthly Income	$1,000
Projected Monthly Expenses	
Mortgage/rent	
Phone (office and cell)	80
Toll-free number	
Postage/shipping	100
Office supplies	15
Owner salary	
Jewelry-making supplies	50
Employee wages	
Employee taxes/benefits	
Advertising/promotion	50
Insurance	100
Legal services	
Accounting services	
Online service	99
Web hosting	8
Merchant account	30
Transportation/maintenance	200
Subscriptions/dues	10
Loan repayment	
Subtotal	742
Miscellaneous expenses (roughly 10% of subtotal)	75
Total Expenses	**$ 817**
Projected Income/Expense Total	**$ 183**

Sample Income & Expenses (Midrange)

Fashion Faire

Projected Monthly Income	**$4,000**
Projected Monthly Expenses	
Mortgage/rent	
Phone (office and cell)	80
Toll-free number	50
Postage/shipping	150
Office supplies	15
Owner salary	
Employee wages	
Employee taxes/benefit	
Inventory	2,000
Advertising/promotion	250
Insurance	100
Legal services	
Accounting services	150
Online service	99
Web hosting	8
Merchant account	75
Travel	250
Transportation/maintenance	200
Subscriptions/dues	60
Loan repayment	300
Subtotal	3,787
Miscellaneous expenses (roughly 10% of subtotal)	380
Total Expenses	**4,167**
Projected Income/Expense Total	**−$167**

Sample Income & Expenses (High End)

Pamplemousse

Projected Monthly Income	**$ 8,000**
Projected Monthly Expenses	
Mortgage/rent	$600
Phone (office and cell)	120
Toll-free number	50
Postage/shipping	100
Office supplies	15
Owner salary	
Employee wages	320
Employee taxes/benefits	
Manufacturing	4,000
Advertising/promotion	500
Insurance	100
Legal services	150
Accounting services	150
Online service	99
Web hosting	8
Merchant account	75
Travel	250
Transportation/maintenance	200
Subscriptions/dues	60
Loan repayment	500
Subtotal	7,297
Miscellaneous expenses (roughly 10% of subtotal)	730
Total Expenses	**$8,027**
Projected Income/Expense Total	**−$27**

Income & Expenses Worksheet

Projected Monthly Income	$
Projected Monthly Expenses	
Mortgage/rent	$
Phone (office and cell)	$
Toll-free number	$
Postage/shipping	$
Office supplies	$
Owner salary	$
Jewelry-making supplies	$
Employee wages	$
Employee taxes/benefits	$
Manufacturing	$
Inventory	$
Advertising/promotion	$
Insurance	$
Legal services	$
Accounting services	$
Travel	$
Online service	$
Web hosting	$
Merchant account	$
Transportation/maintenance	$
Subscriptions/dues	$
Loan repayment	$
Subtotal	$
Miscellaneous expenses (roughly 10% of subtotal)	$
Total Expenses	$
Projected Income/Expense Total	$

Financial Framework

There are several types of monthly, quarterly, and annual reports you'll need to keep your business finances on track. One of the most important is a balance sheet, which lists all assets, liabilities, and capital. It's generated at the end of your accounting period (often month-end) when the books are closed. Equally important is a cash flow statement, which summarizes the operating, investing, and financing activities of your business related to incoming and outgoing cash. But unless you have a secret desire to be a fashion accessories maven by day and Captain Capital at night (or a death wish, depending on how you look at it), it's usually best to leave all these financial wheelings and dealings to a professional. But if you're game to try, crank up your copy of QuickBooks to get advice on how to make the numbers foot (Captain Capital-speak for "add up").

Phone Charges

Even if your business is homebased, it's imperative to have a dedicated phone line for business-related calls. You might want to simply add a second residential landline to your current home service as a way to save cash. A residential line runs $30 to $40 a month, plus the cost of add-on services like voice mail ($12 to $18 extra per month), caller ID ($7.50 for number identification plus an extra $2 for name display) and call waiting ($5). If you're working out of your home and prefer not to publish your number (advisable), you'll pay about $5 more for an unpublished listing.

On the other hand, a business line costs from $150 to as much as $400 a month. If your business is brick-and-mortar, you pretty much have to resign yourself to the higher cost. But you'll get a business listing in the local phone directory and an online listing at Whitepages.com.

But as you probably know, phone service is very competitive, so shop around when you're ready to choose yours. One service we like is Sage Telecom, which offers features like call waiting, caller ID, call forwarding, and 90 minutes of long-distance calling for as little as $25 a month. Another option is Voice over Internet Protocol (VoIP) phone service, which uses the internet to place and receive phone calls and is usually very cost effective. One

Smart Tip

Tip...

If VoIP sounds like a great way to keep your phone expenses down but you need more information to make a decision, check out ConsumerCompare.org, where you'll find a comparison and review of stand-alone internet phone services.

▲

VoIP provider is cable TV giant Comcast (comcast.net), which offers a product called Comcast Digital Voice that gives you unlimited local and long-distance calling, a dozen popular calling features, and voice mail for $40 a month. Other companies that offer VoIP technology include Vonage, which offers calling plans for as low as $24.95 a month (vonage.com); and Packet8, with business plans from $14.99 (packet8.net) and video phone capability (which is a real plus in a visual business like fashion).

If you're planning to have a dedicated fax line (a good idea for taking orders from mom-and-pop retailers who haven't yet entered the 21st century), double your monthly phone bill charges when creating your I&E. Add on other telecommunications devices like a cell phone, a BlackBerry, a push-to-talk phone and/or a pager, and you'll need to adjust those figures upward. For illustration purposes, the sample I&E includes $80 per month for the low-end and midrange businesses and $120 per month for the high-end business, which covers the cost of a landline, a dedicated fax line and one cell phone.

Toll-Free Number

If your business will be internet-based or you think you'll have a lot of retail customers like Reagan Hardy and Emmie Howard of Southern Proper do, a toll-free number is a great service to offer. Toll-free numbers are very inexpensive—usually you'll pay as little as 3.9 cents per minute plus a setup fee—but what they give you in return is priceless; namely, the appearance that you're really interested in offering excellent customer service. We've estimated a cost of $50 per month on the I&E form for the midrange and high-end businesses only.

Office Supplies

Be sure to include a small amount of money for office supplies in your monthly calculations. Mostly you'll need items like stationery, copy/printer paper, and business cards, so as little as $15 a month should be enough to keep you going. Depending on the volume of printing you do, you might need to include enough cash for new toner cartridges ($25 to $80 each) in these calculations.

Postage/Shipping

Virtual stores in particular need to allot funds for shipping, but virtually every type of business described in this book should put some Jacksons or even a few Franklins into this spot on the I&E. Consider whether you'll be shipping samples back and forth to your manufacturer, sending free samples to celebrities or the media, and otherwise promoting your business as a way to determine how much money to allot. Naturally you can reduce this cost by e-mailing news releases and contracts, but not every transaction can be handled virtually, so postage costs are inevitable. The USPS has promised that it will be raising postage rates every May from now until Armageddon, so be sure to check the rate of the day at usps.com.

Many small-business owners prefer to use delivery services like UPS or FedEx for packages. The best reason to choose a delivery service over the USPS is convenience. If the service will come to your door to pick up outgoing packages, that's usually worth the cost. (But to be fair, the USPS will do it, too, so be sure to include it in your fact-finding mission to find the best deal.) Since the low-end sample business is virtual and the midrange business is strictly a reseller, we've included a higher amount for postage on those sample I&Es to reflect the costs of a busy and thriving business.

Wages

While none of the entrepreneurs interviewed for this book initially took a salary in their startup phase, you might want to consider including at least a small stipend in your I&E. This gives you a verifiable wage history, which will be important later when you approach a lender for funding (including for personal expenses like a mortgage or car loan). Also, if you plow all the money back into the business, what fun is that? Take at least a little for yourself as a way to feel as though this self-employment thing has potential. Of course, all you may be able to afford is a cup of coffee or a movie ticket, but hey, you earned it! Alternatively, you can pencil in a phantom salary for yourself on the books. No one says you actually have to spend it.

However, having said all that, the reality is that many small-business owners don't pay themselves at first, so we've chosen only to include the salary for the part-time worker in the high-end business in the I&E calculations.

Speaking of part-time workers, check the local market to see what other small retailers are paying to come up with an equitable wage for your own. You may find that by adding as little as 25 cents an hour to the local average you'll attract more prospects to your business. A good starting point also can be the local minimum wage, but depending on the area, it can be hard to find qualified help at that rate. You'll probably have to play the wage issue by ear and test it until you get it right.

The figure you'll find on the high-end I&E is for a 10-hour-per-week employee at $8 an hour, or approximately $320 per month.

Taxes

You must withhold taxes from the wages of any employee who earns more than $900 per year. These taxes must be sent in to the IRS quarterly, and there are stiff penalties if you miss a deadline. You'll recall from Chapter 11 that there is a whole boxful of taxes that must be withheld from an employee's wages or paid by Ms. or

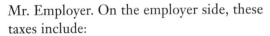
Mr. Employer. On the employer side, these taxes include:

- *FICA (aka Social Security tax):* 6.2 percent
- *Matching portion of Medicare tax:* 1.45 percent
- *Federal unemployment tax:* Another 6.2 percent, although you may be eligible to claim a 5.4 percent credit if you pay state unemployment insurance (see below)
- *State unemployment tax:* the amount varies by state
- *Workers' compensation insurance:* also varies by state

Dollar Stretcher

If your spouse is employed by your business, he's not subject to FUTA tax. However, you'll still have to withhold taxes and send in quarterly Social Security and Medicare tax payments as you would with any other employee. But this only applies if your business is organized as a sole proprietorship.

If you're eligible for the 5.4 percent credit mentioned above, your Federal liability still will be a breathtaking 8.45 percent per employee. So when making your I&E projections, be sure to add in an amount equivalent to 8.45 percent of the employee's wage.

Remember, you can reduce your tax liability significantly by using independent contractors. But beware: Uncle Sam will be watching to make sure you truly have a contractor (who handles his/her own taxes) and not an employee (for whom you'll owe taxes). To understand the distinction and thereby make sure you don't run afoul of the taxman, consult with your accountant, or pick up or download a copy of IRS Publication 15-A, *Employer's Supplemental Tax Guide*, for the full scoop.

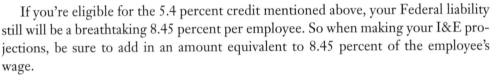

Smart Tip

Always keep your personal and business expenses separate, especially if you're operating as a sole proprietorship. Besides making it easier to get organized around tax time, it's just a more professional way to operate and will help to convince the IRS that you're a legitimate business owner and not a hobbyist.

If you decided to bypass a regular salary, then you don't have to worry about paying personal income taxes on your earnings. But if you do, then Uncle Sam will have his hand out for your Federal "donation," too. The income tax situation for a small-business owner depends on the legal structure of the business. A sole proprietor pays estimated taxes at his or her regular tax rate, as well as a self-employment tax, which consists of the other half of the Social Security and Medicare taxes. An S corporation business owner pays estimated taxes on earnings, even if all revenues are sunk back into the corporation to help it grow. If you have an S corporation, you absolutely must discuss taxing issues with your accountant, because the top corporate tax rate currently is 35 percent and you'll want to make sure you squeeze out every legitimate tax deduction you can to salvage at least some of your earnings.

Estimated taxes on self-employment income are paid quarterly and are based on both earned and anticipated income for the quarter. That's a bit tricky to do because you won't have prior-year earnings figures to help you make an educated guess. Your accountant can help you make reasonable projections that will keep you from incurring the dreaded Underpayment Penalty. Alternatively, just estimate high. You'll get the extra back as a tax refund the following year.

Accounting Services

It bears repeating that you don't want to go it alone when it comes to your business finances. If nothing else, there are so many financial matters that require close and frequent scrutiny that you probably won't have much time left over to design, manufacture and/or sell fashion accessories. So include some funds on your I&E for this important function.

According to Intuit, the maker of TurboTax software, self-employed accountants charge $50 an hour on average. Since your accounting needs will be modest when you launch your business, plan on including about $100 to $150 a month on your I&E, which would cover two to three hours of work on your receivables/payables, tax filings, and other miscellaneous financial tasks. Of course the cost may be higher or lower in your geographic area, so call around to find out the going rate for local accountants. We're assuming that the low-end business owner initially will use financial software like QuickBooks to save money, but $150 has been included for three hours of time on the midrange and high-end business charts.

Legal Services

Unless you'll be designing and manufacturing proprietary accessories, you probably won't need the services of an attorney very often after you start your business. (The cost of startup activities like setting up your business's legal structure, negotiating leases, and handling other startup tasks have already been included in the startup expenses charts in each of the fashion accessories business chapters.) For this reason, we have not included an amount on the I&E for the low-end business.

> **Beware!**
> If a manufacturer refuses to sign your nondisclosure agreement, move on to another company. While a company that really wants to steal your idea will find a way to do it one way or another, don't make it any easier for that to happen by sharing proprietary information before getting a signed nondisclosure agreement.

Protecting Your Turf

While an attorney will happily apply for a trademark for you, you actually can do it yourself quite easily. Just go to the U.S. Patent and Trademark Office (USPTO) website, where you'll find instructions and a very good tutorial on how to proceed: uspto.gov/web/trademarks/workflow/start.htm. Filing fees start at $275.

But if you wish to patent an unusual product, find a patent attorney fast because the process is much more complicated and expensive. Although it's not quite as common to patent a fashion item, if you create something really unusual or novel, it might be worth taking that step since a patent gives the inventor "the right to exclude others from making, using, offering for sale, or selling the invention in the United States or importing the invention into the United States," according to the USPTO.

Be prepared to shell out big bucks for this level of protection: $8,000 to $15,000 just to get a case on file, then another $15,000 to $20,000 to obtain an allowed patent, says David Cornwell, director at the intellectual property law firm Stern, Kessler, Goldstein & Fox PLLC in Washington, DC. But if your product becomes an instant success, there could be millions of dollars at stake, so it pays to consult a patent attorney early on. You can find a list of patent attorneys on the USPTO website at uspto.gov.

But if you think you'll need help, or you want to be extra careful, expect to pay $100 to $450 an hour for assistance.

However, you may need the services of an attorney experienced in intellectual property law if you design products, since someone, somewhere, will probably be waiting in the wings to swoop in and steal your great ideas for his or her own enrichment. The rate for such a specialist varies, but according to Gaebler Ventures, a Chicago-based business incubator, it's not unusual to pay $250 to $275 an hour for expert advice. The high-end business I&E includes a figure of $150 to cover the cost of any phone calls or cease-and-desist letters that might be needed to call off the copycats.

Things you'll want to have an intellectual property law attorney handle for you may include applying for a trademark or a patent on your novel products, and drawing up a confidentiality agreement, known as a nondisclosure agreement (NDA), which you'll give to every manufacturer you talk to about making your accessories.

The latter is important because you'll have to submit detailed information about your products to the manufacturer to get them into production, which leaves open the possibility that the company could steal your idea or manufacture knockoffs.

Insurance

Using the worksheet you filled out in Chapter 7, you can get a good idea of how much you should earmark every month toward your annual insurance premiums. (You'll recall that your first-year premiums have already been covered by startup funds. The figure on your monthly I&E refers to how much you need to save toward next year's premiums.)

Whatever you do, don't skimp on insurance. You can buy a lot of coverage for not a lot of money, which gives you peace of mind. But at the same time, you don't need every type of coverage known to man—or woman. Among the insurance policies you should consider are business owner's insurance, commercial general liability, and property/casualty (for brick-and-mortar stores). A valuable items floater for valuables (either materials or finished products) stored in your home office or valuable article

Beware!
Business liability insurance will not protect you against financial losses—it only protects you against lawsuits by disgruntled vendors or customers. If you feel you need a layer of protection against personal liability, form a corporation or a limited liability corporation (LLC) rather than operating as a sole proprietorship.

in-vault coverage is also a good idea. Since you can usually get a large commercial general liability policy for $500 a year, we've included a high estimate of $100 on each of the I&E statements as a guesstimate of how much you might pay to cover all of your assets.

Internet Service Fees

Typical service charges for monthly internet access are:
- *Standard ISP (dial-up)*: $20 to $25 per month
- *ISDN*: $50 a month, plus $20 to $25 a month for an ISP connection
- *DSL*: $30 to $40 a month
- *Cable modem*: $40 a month, plus basic cable TV service at the very least
- *Broadband (high-speed internet)*: as much as $99 a month

If you have your own website, you'll also have a monthly web hosting charge of $4.95 and up for 2,000MB of space. Since many of the well-known hosts charge $7.95 for hosting and extra features like unlimited e-mails, we've chosen to include a figure of $8 a month on our sample I&Es.

Merchant Account

To accept credit and debit cards, you'll need to establish a merchant account. A merchant account is an electronic clearinghouse that allows you to verify whether a customer's credit is good or if there's sufficient cash in his or her bank account to cover the purchase. To do this in a retail operation like a brick-and-mortar location, you'll need a telephone line to transmit data, as well as a point-of-sale (POS) terminal and a credit card receipt printer or specialized computer software. Then you need a merchant account service to start processing payments.

Fees for merchant accounts vary widely but typically include a retail discount rate on each transaction, which is a fixed percentage deducted from the purchase price by the merchant account provider. This can amount to anywhere from 1.25 percent to 4 percent per transaction. In addition, there's usually a statement fee of about $10 a month, plus a small fee of around 20 cents for each transaction processed. Other typical charges include an initial programming charge, a monthly minimum fee, a "gateway" fee for processing secure online payments, and a charge-back processing fee, which is the fee assessed by credit card companies to cover the cost of transactions disputed by the customer or his/her issuing bank (usually around about $25).

With all these fees, you probably wonder why anyone would be crazy enough to accept credit cards—but of course, it's just the cost of doing business. The good news is the merchant account field is very competitive. Start your search for a good candidate by Googling "merchant accounts." You'll also find several merchant account providers listed in the Appendix that you can explore. For the sake of simplicity, an estimated monthly cost of $30 has been used on the sample I&E statement for the low-end business, and $75 for the midrange and high-end businesses.

There is another viable option that bypasses much of the rigmarole and angst described in the procedure mentioned above, and if you've ever made online purchases you may have heard of it: PayPal. This eBay company is an online payment solution like a merchant account. It's available in 190 markets and 17 currencies, making it easy for you to accept payments worldwide. It's actually more versatile than a merchant account because it's a merchant account and gateway all in one that allows you to accept payments via credit cards, bank accounts (including e-checks), buyer credit, and PayPal account balances. It can be used for many kinds of purchases, including online orders; phone, fax, or mail orders; and online billing. The only thing it *can't* do is process brick-and-mortar retail sales. At least, it can't yet. No doubt that will happen down the road.

The good news about all this is that PayPal takes care of everything for you. There's even a way to process everything virtually so you don't need point-of-sale equipment to process transactions. The bad news is you will pay more with PayPal than you would if you lined up all the merchant account pieces on the board yourself. But frankly, the extra cost may be worth it because you'll skip all the hassles inherent in setting up a regular merchant account and everything that goes with it. For more information and a list of fees, check out PayPal.com.

Inventory

Shipping in a supply of the ready-made or manufactured items you wish to sell will be one of the costliest steps in your startup—as well as one of your most expensive ongoing costs. Because the fashion industry is so vibrant and volatile, it's crucial to keep your product lines fresh and updated. That means you'll have to bring in new merchandise regularly, then run clearance sales to move end-of-season merchandise and make way for those new products.

But that's getting ahead of things. The first thing you must do to determine how much to allocate for monthly inventory acquisitions is some due diligence to determine what the products you'll sell will cost, how much it will cost to get them shipped to you, and so on. For the sake of simplicity, we have included a cost of $2,000 a month on the I&E for the midrange business, which represents the cost of ready-made accessories brought in for resale.

Production Costs

These costs will vary depending on the type of business you're running. For example, a jewelry designer will regularly have to lay in a supply of jewelry-making components like sterling silver and gold jewelry findings, beads, bead wire, gemstones, and other items. A handbag designer will have to hire a pattern maker to create new designs (if he or she is not trained to make patterns), then will pay for production of the handbags. Other common production costs include the cost of 3D computer-aided design (or CAD, which is the "engineering" part of the design process), manufacturing and assembly time, packaging and so on.

Manufacturing costs truly are difficult to estimate for a sample I&E because they're so specific to the type of merchandise being produced. For illustration purposes (so you can see the impact on the monthlies), we've used a figure of $4,000 per month ($48,000 per year) as the production figure for the high-end I&E. On the advice of Liza Sonia Wallach, the Oakland, California, jewelry designer, we've included a figure of $50 (or $600 a year) for the low-end business to represent the ongoing cost of jewelry-making supplies. (She actually spent more on her own startup, but that's another story.) Obviously, there are no manufacturing costs for the midrange business because it is strictly a reseller of wholesale merchandise.

▲

Packaging

If you're manufacturing accessories like handbags, chances are the factory will be able to handle the packaging side of the business for you and will simply include the cost in the overall production price. But if you'll be selling virtually or if you score one of those coveted national retailers as a client, you'll have to take on the packaging duties yourself. Alternatively, you could hire a fulfillment house to box up and send out parcels for you, but often that's too expensive for a small retailer/wholesaler on a shoestring budget.

You'll find a discussion of the types of product packaging jewelry businesses might need in Chapter 2, and the packaging belt, scarf, and hat businesses might use in Chapter 4. (We're assuming that handbag businesses will have packaging materials supplied by the manufacturer.) But the figure on page 193 gives an idea of what wholesale packaging materials cost based on an internet search:

You'll also need some kind of tagging system for your products, both so customers can see the price at a glance and so you can keep track of your inventory. Jewelry tags with a white cotton string attached cost about $17 for a box of 1,000 tags. Larger sizes for scarves and bags run around the same price.

Finally, if you'll be shipping merchandise to online customers, you'll need shipping materials. An easy way to take the guesswork and much, if not all, of the shipping container cost out of the shipping process is to use USPS Priority or Express Mail. Boxes and shipping envelopes are provided free of charge at the post office. You simply fill 'em up and pay a flat rate, which for Priority Mail currently is $9.80 for an 11-by-8.5-by-5.5-inch box up to 70 pounds with no restrictions or distance limitations; or $4.80 for a Priority Mail envelope for up to 70 pounds. You can create mailing labels and pay for postage online, too, and pickup at your home or store is available. The major delivery services like UPS offer similar services as well.

> ## Smart Tip
> **Tip...**
>
> There are many companies on the internet that sell packaging materials suitable for fashion accessories. Google "jewelry box," "ring box," or "wholesale boxes" to find companies to explore. eBay is also a very good source for low-cost packaging materials, usually sold by small-business owners like yourself.

Advertising

Small-business experts usually recommend earmarking 2 to 5 percent of your gross revenues to cover advertising efforts. This can be a little tricky to estimate because you won't have prior-year sales figures available, not to mention your first-year income might be rather modest. For this reason, you should simply set aside a little stash of cash each month—say, $50 to $100 in the case of a homebased business (since

Typical Packaging Costs

Item	Size	Quantity	Price
Economy white paper ring or earring box with lid and cotton filler	$2^1/_2$ x $^1/_2$ x $^7/_8$"	100	$19.90
Economy white paper necklace box with lid and cotton filler	$5^1/_4$ x $3^3/_4$ x $^7/_8$"	100	$31.50
Economy white paper scarf or belt box with lid and cotton filler	8 x $5^1/_2$ x 2"	50	$43.50
"Leatherette" ring box	$2^1/_8$ x $1^7/_8$ x $1^1/_2$"	12 (min. order)	$1.05 each
"Leatherette" earring box	$1^7/_8$ x $1^3/_4$ x $1^3/_8$"	12 (min. order)	$1.05 each
"Leatherette" necklace/bracelet box	8 x 2 x 1"	12 (min. order)	$2.19 each
"Leatherette" necklace box	7 x $4^3/_8$ x $1^3/_4$"	12 (min. order)	$4.35 each
Economy velour-textured jewelry pouch	3 x $3^1/_2$"	48 (min. order)	$ .38 each
Reclosable polybags	3 x 3"	1,000	$10.15
Jewelry tags with white cotton string	$^1/_4$ x $^{11}/_{16}$"	1,000	$16.75

all you're likely to need is line sheets and business cards), $250 for the midrange business, and $500 or more for a brick-and-mortar retailer.

Travel

If you'll be manufacturing your own products or will be purchasing merchandise abroad, you'll need cash to fund a trip or two to your factory. These days, even a trip cross-country is expensive, so if you're traveling to Asia (the world's manufacturing hotbed), be prepared for sticker shock. For instance, at the time of writing a coach airline ticket from New York LaGuardia to Beijing was $1,600 with a 30-day advance purchase. Add in accommodations, transportation, food, and so on, and you could be looking at about $3,000 for a single trip. Naturally, business travel is deductible, but it still takes a big bite out of your budget.

To arrive at a figure you can use in your projections, determine the cost of the airfare, hotel, and per diem for food and incidentals, add about 10 percent to cover miscellaneous expenses, then divide that figure by 12 to arrive at a monthly figure for your worksheet. If you're a retail store owner, you should probably plan on making two trips a year, so you'll need to double that figure. The sample midrange and high-end business I&Es use a figure of $250 ($3,000 over 12 months) to cover the cost of one trip. There is not a figure on the low-end business's I&E because we've assumed its owner will not initially travel outside of her local market.

Dollar Stretcher

The standard mileage rate for business miles established by the IRS in 2008 is 58.5 cents per mile. This applies to cars, vans, pickups and trucks. Keep a mileage log in your vehicle and note your starting and ending mileage every time you drive because the IRS requires written records as proof of miles driven.

Dollar Stretcher

Publications like magazines, newspapers, newsletters, etc., that are related to the fashion industry or business in general are considered part of the cost of doing business and can be included in your monthly business expense calculations. In addition, Uncle Sam will allow you to take those costs as a business deduction when you file your tax return.

Transportation/ Maintenance

If you'll be using your personal vehicle to make sales calls, you'll need to estimate your expenses for your I&E. Expenses you should include are mileage, gasoline, windshield wiper fluid, regular maintenance like tune-ups and oil changes, and bridge and tunnel tolls. If you work in a metropolitan area like Manhattan where there's reliable mass transit, you need to estimate the cost of public transportation like taxis, buses, and the subway. For the sake of simplicity and to reflect the rising cost of gas we've used a figure of $200 for each of the sample businesses.

Membership Dues

Dues for organizations related to your primary business, as well as local business organizations where you can network and share war stories, are all deductible. Tally up the total of all the dues and divide by 12.

Miscellaneous

Include an extra 10 percent of your estimated monthly costs on your I&E for unexpected expenditures or costs that you simply didn't think of as you developed the business.

Receivables

Now that you've gotten past those scary expenses, you can start estimating your receivables. But we won't kid you—even though these are happy projections, as anything related to incoming cash usually is, they can be even harder to predict than expenses. The best way to make financial projections is by basing them on factors like turnover and marketing and customer acquisition. Here's how to approach the process.

Turnover

Because fashion is seasonal, retail experts say clothing stores should have close to four inventory turnovers annually. But while fashion accessories are close relatives of apparel, a turnover factor of two is more reasonable and would allow you to structure your inventory into spring and fall collections. Having said that, here's a formula for projecting your sales for the year as well as your inventory levels, according to retail consultant Anne Obarski:

Sales = average stock x turnover
(starting inventory)

For example, if you have $20,000 worth of inventory times two turnovers, you'll have $40,000 in sales. Once you've determined your planned sales amount, you can determine the amount of stock you need to carry by using this formula:

Stock = sales/turnover

> **Tip...**
>
> ### Smart Tip
> Business-related meal and entertainment expenses incurred while you're out on sales calls or at trade shows generally are deductible on your tax return at a rate of 50 percent. The IRS doesn't require you to have a receipt for expenses under $75, but you still need written records to support any expenses you plan to claim.

So let's say your goal is to do $50,000 in sales the first year. Using this formula, you'll need $25,000 in inventory. A sales goal of $100,000 would require $50,000 in inventory. While that might sound high, it's not beyond the realm of possibility, especially if you're selling wholesale or if you land a big contract.

These calculations work for both brick-and-mortar and virtual operations, although in the case of virtual operations, you'll probably start out with lower inventory levels and have smaller financial returns. That is, unless you're selling big-ticket items like handbags or very high-end jewelry pieces. Then your financial projections could be as high or higher than a retail brick-and-mortar operation.

Marketing/Customer Acquisition

Another way to project sales is to tie the numbers to the way you market your accessories. For example, let's say you plan to advertise a handbag priced at $50 in a fashion publication that has a readership of 100,000. Since research shows that young women are the largest consumers of fashion accessories, let's assume that 50 percent, or 50,000, of the readers of this particular publication are women aged 18 to 30. Finally, let's assume that 3 percent of those readers will actually buy a handbag. (A 3 percent response rate is considered a reasonable response to an ad.) Then your projected sales would be:

$$50,000 \times .03 = 1,500 \times \$50 = \$75,000$$

Of course to achieve those numbers, you'll have to place numerous ads in the publication, but if the end result is sales of $75,000, then the ads will be worth the cost.

If math makes your eyes cross, don't forget that your accountant can help you make reasonable forecasts and projections, then help you figure out how to balance them against your expenses. Sometimes it's better to leave this kind of financial wrangling to the experts.

Finding Financial Resources

Because it's possible to start most of the businesses in this book on a shoestring, chances are you won't need anything more than personal savings and some plastic to foot the bills. But if you're going to become a manufacturing maven, then you'll probably need outside financing. The problem is banks are often reluctant to lend vast sums of money to untried and untested small-business owners, even those who darken their doors with a well-conceived business plan in hand. But not to worry. There are many other options for funding your fashion empire.

Small Bank USA

OK, we did just say that it's hard to get a small-business loan. But it's not impossible because there actually are banks that are small-business-friendly. Your task is to find them. Start by inquiring at community-based banks, which generally have a more relaxed attitude about lending to businesses in their own backyard. One way to find out how open the local bank might be to discussing more than the weather with you is to hunt down a copy of its annual report (usually available in the bank lobby or online). Read it carefully to determine whether the bank has a history of lending to small businesses or minority business owners. If so, that could be the bank to approach. If not, Google "small business banks" for leads. You'll also find that your local SBA office can refer you to prospective banking partners. To find an SBA office near you or for information about the loan programs, go to sba.gov, call the SBA answer desk at 800-U-ASK-SBA (800-827-5722), or e-mail answerdesk@sba.gov.

Small-Business Line of Credit

Another way to squeeze money out of a bank is to apply for a small-business line of credit. Typically these accounts have credit lines up to $100,000, which should be enough to stock up a store or cover manufacturing costs. Both Wells Fargo and Wachovia offer this type of line of credit, as do a million other banks since it's one of the hottest banking products around. Try Googling "small business line of credit" for leads. But be sure to read the fine print when you apply—these types of accounts often have high fees and adjustable interest rates.

Outside Investors

Many entrepreneurs view this as a last resort because, understandably, they'd rather do things their way and keep all the hard-earned profits for themselves. But the reality is, outside investors bring more to the table than just the big bucks—they bring you a golden opportunity to grow the business faster than it would if you try to go it alone with your limited resources.

You don't have to give away the store, so to speak, nor do you have to carve up your business when you bring investors aboard. Depending on your tolerance for sharing, you

> ## Tip...
> ### Smart Tip
> Even if you don't need any outside financing when you launch your business, it's a good idea to apply for a business line of credit at your bank. Use it as a source of short-term cash that you can tap into when cash flow is slow or an unexpected expense pops up.

can offer them a piece of the business on an ongoing basis, structure a deal that gives them a percentage of the profits, or arrange for short-term loans at a reasonable interest rate, thus returning the business to you as soon as possible. Family members and friends are obvious sources of this type of funding, but if you do tap into then, be sure to structure the loans as legitimate business transactions, with a schedule of regular payments and interest charges in writing. That prevents future misunderstandings that can result in the loss of a treasured friend or irreparable damage to family relationships.

New York jewelry entrepreneur Ruta Fox had to turn to friends and family to save her business. After her signature product, the Ah Ring, appeared in *O, The Oprah Magazine*, she had tons of orders, but not enough capital to buy the rings from overseas. At one point, she needed $30,000 by the next day to fulfill orders, and had to "dial for dollars," as she puts it. She asked for and received $10,000 from the attorney who incorporated her business, another $10,000 from a friend's mother ("I thought her offer was just cocktail party chatter," Fox says), more funds from a friend who tapped into a 401(k) plan, and surprisingly to her, the rest from the Bank of Mom, the woman who "gave me $25 for my birthday my entire life but wired the money I needed overnight," Fox says.

Although this type of arrangement can work, it's usually better to seek financing partnerships with strangers than with loved ones, and there are plenty of people out there who might be interested in investing in your company if you can give them a reasonable assurance that they'll receive a return on their investment. For leads to potential investors, start with the SBA, which maintains a list of small-business investment companies on its website that includes everyone from venture capitalists, who routinely invest $1 million or more, to companies that specialize in lending to smaller businesses like yours.

Finally, an angel investor could be the answer to your prayers. These types of investors are high-net-worth individuals who invest in new entrepreneurial ventures, usually when they're in the earliest stages, and take equity in the business in return for providing a financial cushion. Because they're usually successful entrepreneurs themselves, angels also are a great source of advice and wisdom you can count on since they'll be just as eager as you are to make your business a success.

To find an angel investor or network, consult with your professional advisors and other business associates. Your local chamber of commerce may also be able to provide you with names. Alternatively, you can Google "angel investors" and the name of your city for leads, or visit the Gaebler Ventures website at gaebler.com/angel-investor-networks.htm for a list of angel networks by state.

The Bottom Line

Despite all the big numbers tossed around in this chapter, you'll probably find that the cost to run your business every month will be fairly manageable. Of course all bets are off if you're planning to manufacture your own products or you'll be selling accessories from a brick-and-mortar location. Then you'll have higher monthly liabilities. But with the right business advice, sufficient operating funds and enough enthusiasm, you can make this work. The reward will be a business you can be proud of and a career you'll find both exciting and satisfying. You can't ask for more than that.

Finishing
Touches

So there you have it—all the background information you need to establish your own fashion accessories business. What lies ahead of you is the sheer joy and genuine fun of creating the products, marketing them, and seeing your fashion dreams come true. But at the same time, now is a good time to do a reality check because the fact is, small-business owners face a lot of challenges on the way to success.

According to the SBA, two-thirds of new firms survive at least two years, and about 44 percent survive at least four. That's the half-full view. The half-empty reality is that 34 percent of new businesses don't survive the first couple of years, while 56 percent give up the ghost around the four-year mark. Your task, then, is to make the right moves so your business is among the happy statistics.

Factors that Hinder Success

Small-business experts like the SBA believe that businesses fail for a number of predictable reasons. First and foremost, poor management skills can sink a business fast. So can a lack of sufficient operating capital, which is especially important for keeping operations afloat in the lean early days. A lack of proper planning is also deadly to a new business, because without a well-conceived business plan and contingency plan for dealing with the normal ups and downs of business operations, it's impossible to counteract them effectively. Finally, a business that doesn't have a

---

Don't Worry, Be Happy

Winston Churchill said, "Courage is going from failure to failure without losing enthusiasm." As a small-business owner, you're going to need a lot of courage. Courage to try new things. Courage to try again when those new things don't work out. And courage to carry on when the economy wanes, your customers are slow to pay, and you're not sure where you're going to get the funds to pay for the merchandise you desperately need to fulfill orders.

Naturally, you have to address all these issues and the thousands more that will crop up in the life cycle of your business. But there's something else you need to make all these pieces fall into place: a positive attitude.

Research shows that optimistic people are more successful, better adjusted, healthier, and just plain happier than those whose glasses are half empty. So when confronted with challenging situations, use positive words to characterize them, as in "I can do it," rather than "I hope I can do it." Banish negative thoughts. Visualize yourself completing new projects successfully and triumphantly before you start them. The mind is a powerful tool—use it to imbue yourself with a sense of purpose, determination, and hope.

May all your dreams of happy self-employment come true!

---

website is more prone to financial disaster because people today rely on the internet to help them do business better, smarter, and faster, which means you have to be out there extending a cyber handshake when they're ready to make or are thinking about making a deal.

Then there are the unique problems faced by retailers and wholesalers alike. Your operations will be heavily influenced by outside and often uncontrollable factors like economic conditions, rising inventory costs (especially due to increasing energy prices), high overhead, and the astronomical cost of employees.

These are just some of the reasons why, throughout this book, we have so strongly and so frequently recommended that you hire business professionals like an attorney and an accountant to assist you with business operations. It's not only the best way to ensure business success, it's also the surest way to make sure you have time to do what you love most—to design and/or sell fashion accessories. And that, of course, is the point of this whole business startup exercise. Everything else should be viewed as a means to that end.

Beware!
According to the SBA, many business owners try to tough it out when they're faced with financial problems—then find out it's too late to save their company when they finally do ask for help. If you start seeing signs of financial stress, call the SBA or SCORE for help. The advice is free, and it could save your business.

Life Lessons

But, of course, when you're excited about the prospect of launching your own business and actually making money doing something you love, it's easy to lose sight of the big picture and make hasty decisions that can hold you back, as the entrepreneurs interviewed for this book can attest. For example, Reagan Hardy and Emmie Howard, the Atlanta men's accessories entrepreneurs, readily admit that they should have obtained some firsthand retail experience to find out what it's like to be on the other side of the selling experience and to gain insight into the men's fashion industry. "That would have been very beneficial for us in the beginning as we started to create relationships," Hardy says.

Donna von Hoesslin, the California belt and jewelry designer, agrees. "I think I would have been more successful with sales if I had been a salesperson first," she admits.

David Kulaas, the Colorado scarf designer, would have tried to target his early sales efforts better. "I learned by trial and error," he says. "I would wander into stores with my eyes closed and stumble around. I didn't know anything about sales or the business of women's fashion, but I still had visions of walking into Nordstrom and selling there right away. Now I can tell right away if the store is a prospect when I walk

in by doing something as simple as looking to see if it carries scarves, then looking at the price range."

Then there are those mavericks who bypass conventional wisdom altogether, as Ruta Fox, the New York ring retailer, did. While she now definitely believes in the value of having regular business advisors like accountants, in the early days she got advice from an unusual source. "I have a friend in Los Angeles who reads [tarot] cards, and she told me, 'You're going to do something humongous,'" Fox says. "She told me to get 250 rings. Unfortunately, I didn't have the money at the time to do it."

Eventually she did get the money, and the rest is history. But she stands by the value of that early advice. "I haven't had a failure [in my career] because I had my psychic to guide me!" she says with a laugh.

The Final Analysis

You don't need your own psychic to know that hard work, determination, dedication, and just plain heart will go a long way toward making you successful. So will being in the right place at the right time. But you don't have to wait for good fortune to smile on you—you can make your own good luck by promoting your accessories aggressively. Send out news releases often to highly targeted audiences. Try pay-per-click advertising. Put samples in the hands of influential buyers and media types.

And talk, talk, talk about your products because you never know who's listening. That's how Hardy and Howard came to the attention of an executive for one of the largest media conglomerates in the Southeast. Actually, Howard sat next to the executive's *wife* on a flight from Atlanta to New York after she and Hardy attended their first clothing show in the Big Apple. When the woman found out what the budding entrepreneurs did for a living, she was not only very impressed— she introduced them to her husband when they reached baggage claim. "Less than two weeks later, we received a call from a newspaper editor who wanted to interview us for a story," Hardy says. "Little did we know that the woman we think of as the 'Lady on the Plane' would help propel [us to] success."

But while it helps to get that kind of break, the success of your fashion accessories business ultimately will be up to you. According to Liza Sonia Wallach, the Oakland, California, jewelry designer, all you have to do is: "Do what you love, focus on being the best to a select client base, and make the best product out there."

We couldn't have said it better ourselves.

Appendix
Fashion Accessories Resources

They say you can never be too rich or too thin. While these could be argued, we believe you can never have enough resources. Therefore, we're giving you a wealth of sources to check into, check out, and harness for your own personal information blitz.

These sources are tidbits—ideas to get you started on your research. They are by no means the only sources out there, and they should not be taken as the ultimate answer. We have done our research, but businesses do tend to move, change, fold, and expand. As we have repeatedly stressed, do your homework. Get out there and start investigating!

Art and Craft Show Listings

Art and Craft Shows.net
artandcraftshows.net

Crafts Fair Online
craftsfaironline.com

Festival Network Online
festivalnet.com

Attorney Referrals and Information

American Bar Association
abanet.org

Find an Attorney
findanattorney.com

Lawyers.com
lawyers.com

Martindale-Hubbell Law Directory
(800) 526-4902
martindale.com

Blogs

Let's Talk Fashion
fashion-schools.org/blog/

See Pretty Things
seeprettythings.com

ShoppingBlog.com
shoppingblog.com/fashionaccessories/

Sparkle Plenty
divinediamonds.com

Wholesale Fashion Jewelry and Accessories blog
awnol.com/wholesale-fashion-blog/

Books

1001 Ways to Create Retail Excitement
Edgar A. Falk
Prentice Hall Press

Retail Business Kit for Dummies
Rick Segel
For Dummies

Specialty Shop Retailing
Carol L. Schroeder
Wiley

Start Your Own Clothing Store and More
Charlene Davis
Entrepreneur Press

Business Software

Intuit
intuit.com

Microsoft
microsoft.com

Demographic Information

American Demographics
(212) 210-0100
demographics.com

U.S. Census Bureau
census.gov

Design Software

Amethyst Handbag Library
thehandbagresource.com

Illustrator CS4
adobe.com

Photoshop CS4
adobe.com

Employee and Supplier Issues

Better Business Bureau
bbb.org

U.S. Department of Labor
dol.gov

Fashion Accessories Business Owners

Ruta Fox
Divine Diamonds
divinediamonds.com
info@divinediamonds.com

Reagan Hardy and Emmie Howard
Southern Proper
(404) 805-3825
southernproper.com
Reagan@southernproper.com

Donna von Hoesslin
Betty Belts and Betty B.
bettybelts.com
surfchick@mac.com

Liza Sonia Wallach
LIZASonia
(415) 845-1044
LizaSonia.com
liza@lizasonia.com

Fashion Industry Associations

Accessories Council
accessoriescouncil.com

Footwear Distributors and Retailers of America
(202) 737-5660
fdra.org

National Fashion Accessories Association
(212) 947-3424
accessoryweb.com
info@accessoryweb.com

Intellectual Property Protection

U.S. Copyright Office
uscopyright.gov

U.S. Patent and Trademark Office
uspto.gov

Manufacturers Information

The National Register
(213) 622-3601
thenationalregister.com

Merchandise Marts

AMC Inc./AmericasMart
(404) 220-3000
americasmart.com

Charlotte Merchandise Mart
(704) 333-7709
carolinasmart.com

Dallas Market Center
(214) 655-6100
dallasmarketcenter.com

▲

Denver Merchandise Mart
(303) 292-6278
denvermart.com

Giftcenter & Jewelry Mart
(415) 861-7733
gcjm.com

Indianapolis Gift Mart
(317) 546-0719

Kansas City Gift Mart
(913) 491-6688
kcgiftmart.com

The L.A. Mart
(213) 749-7911
lamart.com

The Market Center
(212) 686-1203

The Merchandise Mart
(800) 677-6278
merchandisemart.com

**Miami International
Merchandise Mart**
(305) 261-2900
miamimart.net

Minneapolis Gift Mart
(612) 932-7200
mplsgiftmart.com

The New York Merchandise Mart
(212) 686-1203
41madison.com

Northeast Market Center
(978) 670-6363
thegiftcenter.com

Pittsburgh Expomart
(412) 856-8100
pghexpomart.com

Seattle Gift Center
(206) 767-6800
pacificmarketcenter.com

Southern Clothing Market
(704) 366-3654; fax (704) 366-3651
mensapparelclub.com
charlotte@mensapparelclub.com

Merchant Accounts

Capital Merchant Solutions Inc.
(877) 495-2419, (309) 452-5990;
fax (866) 313-0716
chargem.com
info@capital-merchant.com

Credit Card Processing Services
(888) 246-2775, (215) 489-7878;
fax (215) 489-7880
ccps.biz
Kevin@ccps.biz

InfoMerchant
(800) 632-4605
infomerchant.net

Merchant Accounts Express
(888) 845-9457, (603) 262-1210
merchantexpress.com

**Network Solutions Merchant
Accounts**
(800) 838-9699
merchantaccounts.networksolutions.com
sales@bscworldwide.com

Total Merchant Services
(888) 871-4558; fax (423) 843-9864
merchant-account-4U.com
info@21cr.com

Office Equipment (Phones)

Hello Direct
(800) 444-3556
HelloDirect.com

Office Supplies, Forms, and Stationery

Mark Art Productions
business-stationers.com

Office Depot
officedepot.com

Office Max
officemax.com

Office Shop Direct
officeshopdirect.com

Rapidforms
(800) 257-8354
rapidforms.com

Staples
staples.com

Online Postage

Pitney Bowes
pitneyworks.com

Stamps.com
stamps.com

USPS
usps.com

Zazzle
zazzle.com

Packaging Resources

Fetpak Inc.
(800) 883-3872; fax (888) 329-4600
fetpack.com

Midatlantic Packaging
midatlanticpackaging.com

Printing Resources

ColorPrintingCentral
(800) 309-3291
colorprintingcentral.com

Postcard Press
(800) 957-5787
postcardpress.com

Print Industry Exchange LLC
(703) 631-4533; fax (703) 729-2268
printindustry.com
info@printindustry.com

Printing for Less
(800) 930-6040
printingforless.com
info@printingforless.com

Print Quote USA
(561) 451-2654; fax (561) 725-0246
printquoteusa.com

Promotion Xpress
(888) 310-7769, (510) 357-0238;
fax (510) 357-2088
proxprint.com
support@proxprint.com

PSPrint
(800) 511-2009; fax (510) 444-5369
psprint.com

Publications

Apparel News
apparelnews.net

Bead & Button
beadandbutton.com

DNR
dnrnews.com

Global Sources/Fashion Accessories
globalsources.com

Lustre
lustremag.com

Sunshine Artist
sunshineartist.com

Threads
taunton.com/threads/

Woman's Wear Daily
wwd.com

Small Business Development/ Entrepreneurship Organizations

Ladies Who Launch
ladieswholaunch.com

National Federation of Independent Business
NFIB.com

SBA
sba.gov

SCORE
score.org

Small Business Development Centers
sba.gov

Tax Advice, Help, and Software

H&R Block
handrblock.com

Internal Revenue Service
irs.ustreas.gov

Intuit TurboTax for Business
intuit.com

Trade Shows

Accessorie Circuit
enkshows.com

AccessoriesTheShow
(212) 710-7406
accessoriestheshow.com

FAME
(877) 904-FAME
fameshows.com

Florida Fashion Focus
(888) 249-1377
floridafashionfocus.com

The Haberdashery Group
(803) 254-9738; fax (803) 254-9774
haberdasherygroup.com,

MAGIC
(810) 593-5000
show.magiconline.com

Trade Show Displays

Airworks Displays & Booths
airwork.com

BMA
bmadisplay.com

Event Solutions
eventsolutions.com

New World Case Inc.
portablebooths.com

Pinnacle Displays
pinnacledisplays.com

Siegel Display Products
siegeldisplay.com

SmartExhibits.com
smartexhibits.com

Web Hosting/Domain Names

Domain.com
domain.com

EarthLink
earthlink.net

GoDaddy.com
godaddy.com

HostMonster
hostmonster.com

SBC Webhosting.com
webhosting.com

Webhosting.com
webhosting.com

Yahoo!
yahoo.com

Wholesale Product Directories

Clothing Wholesale Manufacturer.com
clothingwholesalemanufacturer.com

Glossary

Blog: web log, an online newsletter or journal; can have more than one author.

Branding: a strategy to get customers to remember your company or product in a favorable way.

Carbon footprint: a measure of humankind's impact on the environment in terms of greenhouse gases and calculated by carbon dioxide emissions.

Chargeback: a pervasive retail practice in which the buyer charges the seller a penalty for anything he/she feels wasn't done right when products are delivered.

Click-and-brick: a company that operates both online (click) and out of a physical location (brick); also known as click-and-mortar.

Click-through: the process of clicking on an online advertisement and being directed to an advertiser's website.

Contract manufacturer: a company that's hired to manufacture products that are marketed and sold by another company.

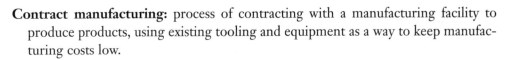

Contract manufacturing: process of contracting with a manufacturing facility to produce products, using existing tooling and equipment as a way to keep manufacturing costs low.

Copyright: protection for intellectual property like artistic work (including fashion accessories designs); a copyright lasts for the life of the creator plus 70 years.

Corporation: a separate legal entity distinct from its owners.

DBA (doing business as): refers to your legal designation once you've selected a business name different from your own and registered it with your local or state government.

Dedicated telephone line: a phone line used for a single purpose, such as for a fax machine or internet data line.

Demographics: the primary characteristics of your target audience, such as age, gender, ethnic background, income level, education level, and home ownership.

Domain name: the address of an internet network (for example, entrepreneur.com); see also URL.

Drop: when referring to handbags or bags, the distance from the top of the handle to the purse; for example, a handbag with an 18-inch strap has a 9-inch drop.

Drop-shipping: sending merchandise from the manufacturer directly to the customer.

E-mail blast: an electronic mailing sent to a large mailing list; if wanted, it's an e-mail blast; if not, it's spam.

Executive summary: brief document at the beginning of a report like a business plan that summarizes its contents.

FAQs: frequently asked questions.

Fashion stylist: the person responsible for gathering the clothing, shoes, and accessories needed for a fashion photo shoot.

FOB: initials for freight on board (or sometimes free on board), meaning that the price of the goods being shipped includes delivery at the seller's expense to a specified point; for example, FOB China means the factory pays the freight as far as the Chinese port from where it will be shipped, while FOB Los Angeles would mean that the seller will ship the product to the Port of L.A. at its expense.

Freelancer: a self-employed person who works on a project or contract basis to produce written materials or artwork for advertisements, brochures, or other printed materials (including news releases).

Freight on board: *See FOB.*

Hardwall booth: booth constructed with plywood or similar material as opposed to a booth formed by drapery only.

Inline mall store: a store located inside a mall.

Intellectual property: anything you create out of your own mind, which in the fashion industry might include designs, inventions, names, and images.

Jewelry findings: clasps, jump rings, pin backings, and other "hardware" used to create jewelry.

Jump ring: an all-purpose round or oval connector ring used in jewelry making to connect charms, chains, fasteners and other things to jewelry items like bracelets and necklaces.

Keystone markup: a retail term that refers to the practice of doubling the wholesale price to determine the retail price.

Keyword advertising: paying for placement and click-throughs of keywords on the results list of a web page; keywords usually appear in a banner ad or at the side of a search results page and direct surfers to the advertiser who bid for the right to place it there.

Keywords: search terms or phrases that appear in the text of a web page or in meta tags that match words used by people who are surfing the internet via a search engine.

Lead time: amount of time from when an order is placed to when merchandise is received.

Line sheet: merchandise information sheet given to retail customers that provides information like size, item number, and price, along with a drawing or a photo of the merchandise.

LLC: Limited liability company.

Logo (or logotype): an identifying symbol used by organizations (as in advertising).

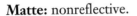

Matte: nonreflective.

Meta tag: a coding statement in HTML language that describes the contents of a web page, including its title, description, and keywords, among other things; usually appears at the top of a web page as part of the heading.

Mission statement: a brief summary telling who your company is, what you do, what you stand for, and why you do it.

Navigation: cyber directions given on a website to help the user to move easily from one page to another.

News release: a one-to-two-page article about some positive aspect of your business meant to generate favorable publicity; also known as a "press release."

Partnership: a business owned equally by two or more persons, or partners.

PPC: Pay per click; refers to the price advertisers are willing to pay every time someone clicks on their keywords on a search results page.

Press kit: a packet that contains publicity and sales materials about a company and its services.

Right of publicity: a person's legal right to control and profit from the use of his or her name or likeness; many states (including California) recognize right of publicity by statute or case law.

Sole proprietorship: a business owned by one person.

Storefront business: a business located on a main street, possibly on the ground floor of a commercial business, that shares common walls with the businesses on either side of it.

Strike-off: manufacturing term for a sample of printed fabric that's provided so the color and style can be checked before printing.

Title tag: the title of a web document, created as an HTML (meta) tag and inserted in the top line of a web browser.

Trademark: a name, logo, or other device that differentiates one product from another and ensures that it's unique.

URL: uniform resource locator, or the internet address locator.

Vegan leather: artificial leather substitute favored by vegetarians.

VoIP: acronym for Voice over Internet Protocol, a type of technology for delivering voice conversations over the internet.

Zoning variance: a one-time exception to a municipal zoning ordinance; for example, you may need zoning variance to be able to operate a business out of your home.

Index